easy MONEY SMART$

JIM W. MATHE

Creator of EASY MONEY SMARTS Seminars

iUniverse, Inc.
Bloomington

Easy Money Smarts

iUniverse books may be ordered through booksellers or by contacting:

iUniverse
1663 Liberty Drive
Bloomington, IN 47403
www.iuniverse.com
1-800-Authors (1-800-288-4677)

ISBN: 978-1-4620-3541-0 (sc)
ISBN: 978-1-4620-3542-7 (hc)
ISBN: 978-1-4620-3543-4 (e)

Library of Congress Control Number: 2011911576

Printed in the United States of America

iUniverse rev. date: 07/01/2011

Dedicated to those who have helped me achieve my goals and to those I have helped along the way.
And to Nora, for her invaluable help and support.

EASY MONEY SMARTS

CONTENTS

INTRODUCTION

Not all rich people start life wealthy – I certainly did not. I was partially raised by the Children's Aid Society in Canada and started out with nothing. Life was a struggle but I learned how to survive, and more importantly, how to financially succeed. I started gaining financial security by buying and selling real estate. Later, I moved on to do the same with several businesses, franchises, and computer investing programs and yes, I even played the stock market.

Now I want to share what I've learned. Writing this book is my way of helping others: I can guide you in the right direction so you will avoid the pitfalls I encountered. Making people's lives better – not just financially but inwardly – is as rewarding for me as any of my investments.

My program for financial success is not complicated. It is doable for any person who wants to get ahead in life. You will start slowly and realistically. I will show you how to get on the right road even if you are behind in your payments or have poor credit. I'll tell you how to get rid of bad debt and how to save – in ways that you might not have thought possible.

Dedication and sincerity is more important than cash. It doesn't matter how little money you have – what's important is that you START the process of becoming financially successful. Don't be embarrassed by the small amount of cash you might presently have. I'll show you fundamental steps for putting money in your pocket, and keeping it there.

I prescribe a common sense approach, not a 'get rich quick' scheme. My *Easy Money Smarts* (EMS) program is realistic and will get you on top without risk, pain or suffering.

Easy Money Smarts will show you the good and bad side of all kinds of investments. You'll discover which ones have the least risk and most potential. So you'll start to make good financial decisions, tailored to your personality and situation.

I will help you succeed but it will require dedication, diligence and persistence on your part. Managing money is something you will need to get used to doing. You must be convinced that you need to do this for yourself and your family. Once you are on track and making money you will see a huge difference in your life because you will be happier, more emotionally satisfied, and it will show in your whole being. People will see the difference in you. Your home life and health will make you feel great.

I have attempted to put everything in simple everyday language. You can visit my web site *(www.easymoneysmarts.com)* and email me. Once you learn – and practice – my simple rules you will find that your life will change in a positive and unbelievable way.

There are many things in life to be thankful for. I hope this book will be one of them.

Time is money. Money is time. Let's get you started!

Jim W. Mathe

CHAPTER ONE

WHO ARE YOU? (REALLY!)

"No one remains quite what he was,
once he recognizes himself."

Thomas Mann, 1875-1955 German novelist

The first step to financial wealth is to know yourself – for real.

No joking, no kidding, no stories – nothing but the truth and the whole truth. If you are not going to be honest with yourself this book will not help you.

What are you afraid of when it comes to making or investing money? Is it your job, partner, health, family, poor credit, fear of scam artists? Or do you fear making a bad deal or decision? Maybe you lack the confidence to make a financial commitment, or perhaps you believe you don't have enough money to become financially successful.

These are valid considerations. But what if I help you overcome your fears? And find out that you don't need a lot of money (or any!) to get started.

Often the biggest obstacle in moving ahead is our selves. Some figment of our imagination has us on the run, and keeps telling us not to try – or that we will not make it anyway, so why bother? Do you have the desire to kill these fears? Knowledge builds confidence and confidence kills fear (and that's why you have this book).

So let's talk about your fears and get them out in the open. Take a look at them honestly and deal with them one at a time.

Let's take a look at your job. Are you happy with it? Does it give you personal satisfaction? Does it give you enough money to live like you really want to? Is it a dead end career? Are your peers really helpful or courteous? Are you appreciated? Well, I can tell you that not all my past jobs were pleasant BUT the one thing that kept me focused and extremely positive was I knew that I was getting ahead.

Good returns from my investments made me happy inside and I knew that eventually I would fulfill my dreams (and drive the car I always wanted!). I found that if I stayed focused on my investments and treated them like my best friend, a lot of trivial things in life would not matter so much.

I am here to tell you that you only need to think positively, and believe in yourself. I will not let you make poor investments or decisions. You are no longer alone, and don't need to feel afraid that you will do something wrong and lose everything you own.

Another obstacle that might be holding you back is thinking you don't have enough money to really get involved in saving and investing. There is something in life that is even worse than fear, and that is regret. Yes, REGRET.

Do you want to live the rest of your life regretting that you never really tried because you let your mind tell you could not do it? Do you want to take this to your grave? The days, months and years will fly by and one day you will wish you had tried even a little to make saving and investing work for you – instead of standing on the sidelines and watching life go by. Time is one of the most precious things we have. Use it well and you will reap the rewards. This is key to your personal success.

Take even the

smallest amount of money

that you can afford

and I will show you how to invest

and

start making money

TODAY!

Investing can be likened to building a house for you and your family. Once you dig the hole in the ground for the solid foundation the next steps get easier and take shape over time. Believe me, building your financial house is every bit as exciting as building the real thing. You will want to visit the site every day to personally monitor its growth. Even on days when nothing happens, it is still uplifting just to stand there and see your progress.

It's a motivating and unbelievable feeling to know you are on the path to success. It will make you feel like a different person! Happy and content regardless of what kind of day you are having. The best part of financial success is that you can pass it on to your family or anyone you choose – helping them be content and stress-free about money.

You need to think like the rich and act like the rich by changing your outlook on money. You need have your money work for you, not you working for the money. Just like the rich. And it's all in your attitude towards money.

If somebody earns a hundred thousand dollars a year they are considered to be doing very well in their life – even considered successful. But the truth of the matter is that many of these people do not have any savings or investments. They are often over financed with big mortgage payments, expensive car payments and all the monthly bills.

On the other hand the person earning forty thousand dollars a year who can save three thousand dollars is way ahead of the hundred thousand dollar a year guy.

If you can't take a little discomfort now, you will be feeling a lot of discomfort later in life.

Remember, the one thing **worse**

than fear is **regret.**

Let me tell you about

something very simple that changed my life.

MY HUMBLE PEBBLE

Once I was told to pick out a token – a little stone – and always carry it in my pocket. This pebble was to represent all the good fortune in my life, and every morning I was to look at it and give thanks for my good health, my wife and children, my worldly possessions, my job and everything else in my life that was wonderful.

At first this humble pebble idea seemed dumb, but it started to grow on me and I began looking forward to seeing it. When I paid for my lunch it was with my loose change and it became a silent reminder of the reasons to be happy with my life. When I bought gas, or flowers, or went to the local variety store it reminded me of what I was grateful for. Holding it in my hand seemed to give me strength and determination to get through any difficult situation.

After many years I still carry my humble pebble – a polished and colorful small stone. It has little value to others, but to me it stands for everything I own. When my brother died I held it in my hand for most of the day and I believe it helped me remember the good and happy things about his life. I not only felt close to him, but I also felt a strong appreciation for everything else in my life.

I highly recommend that you find a humble pebble and carry it with you at all times. It will give you amazing inner strength.

PUT YOUR DREAMS ON PAPER

We all have dreams. Some are bigger than others. But we all dream about what we would do if we won the lottery – yes, all that money – WOW! Financial freedom at last.

Well, let's take your personal dreams and put them on paper. Yes, write about them, draw them, or cut out pictures of what you dream about to create a vision board. Cut out that awesome holiday picture, and that fancy high priced car you always talk about and place it on your vision board next to your holiday picture. Now imagine the really big house and anything else your heart desires and place a picture of them on the board. This is your vision board. Place it somewhere where you will see it everyday – so you don't loose sight of your dream.

Your dream is everything and some people will achieve it quicker than others. But that's alright because you have to do it your own way. Everyone can feel happy knowing they are getting closer to their idea of success day by day. Never put your vision board out of sight because it goes hand in hand with your humble pebble. Both will reinforce your dream every time you see or touch them – and they will help you stay focused and on course, especially through trying times.

Look at your vision board every morning before you go to work and think positively about your future – keep telling yourself you will soon have the items on your board. Hold your token in your hand, rub it gently as you think about the gifts you already have – your family, your health, etc, and what is yet to come into your life.

Here's an example of a vision board. It shows a fancy car, a dream home, cash, a vacation to some tropical place, creative ideas, the wish to upgrade education and inspirational words. Nice!

Your vision board should represent all the things you want in life. Your dream come true! You can include anything your heart desires. The more personal, the better. Dream your own dream!

You will want to make your vision board attractive because YOU WILL BE LOOKING AT IT DAILY. The more attractive the board the stronger your feelings will be around achieving your goals.

This will be an important part of your new life – don't just throw something together, put some time and effort into it. Remember it's your life – it's your dream. Make it attractive so it inspires and motivates you.

Your vision board is your

stepping stone to fulfilling

your dreams.

THE LAW OF ATTRACTION

Many people want to get rich quick. Get over it. It does not happen except for lotteries, and what are the odds that it's going to be you? You can have wealth, but it does take time and some effort. Success will not just fall in your lap. You have to make it happen. And once it does start to happen you will notice everything in your life changing for the better as well. It is referred to as the law of attraction and it works! Set your goals and tune your mind with a focused passion to get you there and everything else will follow. That's the magic. People who have followed these steps know they work, and once that ball starts rolling it doesn't stop.

Your wish is your mind's command. If you say you can't reach your goal, your mind will grant you your wish! That's right – you won't achieve it.

You are what you think about. If you think about not having money – you won't have any. Focus on what you really to do want instead of what you don't want. Focusing on what you don't want will only attract more of the same. Focusing on what you do want will attract it. Making a personal vision board will help.

The good energy that your positive attitude gives off will cause positive actions to happen in your favour. For instance, if you walk into the bank to do a transaction with a cheerful smile and greet everyone in a pleasant and happy way, you will receive that same energy back in the form of more smiles and greetings from everyone there. This is a positive reaction to your first action. People who do this day after day will always get positive reactions in their favour. People looking at them will always say "Wow! That person is always smiling, in a good mood, and always very nice to talk to. He or she must have horseshoes in their back pocket because it seems that everything they touch seems to turn out right." Well, guess what? It has very little to do with luck, but only appears so. I believe that a combination of positive thinking along with positive actions pay off in positive rewards.

When you are positive, things will change in your favour. They have to, because positive energy gives off more positive energy. (Just as negative energy gives off more negative energy.)

Try to avoid people with negative attitudes. Like a bad cold, they are often hard to get rid of! They will bring you down, and keep you there for quite a while.

Energy flows where your mind goes. If it's negative, then the attraction will be negative. If you focus on the positive, then the attraction will be positive. Constantly think about your end results with a positive mind. Be thankful for the things you already have and for where you are. And be positive no matter what your day is like. Just keep smiling!

Whatever you believe, you will attract.

"Whether you think you can or not – you are always right."
Henry Ford

*To build a solid foundation for wealth **you must set your goals and be diligent** about wanting to obtain them.*

SET YOUR GOALS ... AND COMMIT TO THEM!

Your plan does not have to be grand or elaborate – better to keep it simple and obtainable, so you won't get discouraged or frustrated. Your goals need to be something you can live with every day. It will be a wonderful experience to be able to see your plan grow from a seed into a flower. Exhilarating, motivating, and humbling all at the same time.

What do you really want? What's on your vision board? Affirm your dreams over and over (and over!) – get emotionally involved.Really start believing that you can make your dreams come true! Security comes from inside you. Write down the answers to the following questions. Beside each answer, state WHEN you would like to achieve your goal by.

1. What is your passion? What excites you? What motivates you?

2. What are your life's financial goals? Do you want to buy a house, car, apartment building, stocks, or go on a super holiday? Do you want to help out your family financially? Provide university or college education for your children?

Hop on board!
Let's start this journey!

EASY MONEY SMARTS
TRAIN RIDE TO SUCCESS

EASY MONEY SMARTS
MY PASSIONS ARE:

1.

2.

3.

4.

EASY MONEY SMARTS

MY FINANCIAL GOALS ARE:

1. GOAL:

I PLAN TO ACHIEVE THIS BY:

2. GOAL:

I PLAN TO ACHIEVE THIS BY:

3. GOAL:

I PLAN TO ACHIEVE THIS BY:

4. GOAL:

I PLAN TO ACHIEVE THIS BY:

5. GOAL:

I PLAN TO ACHIEVE THIS BY:

6. GOAL:

I PLAN TO ACHIEVE THIS BY:

EASY MONEY SMARTS

MY FEARS ABOUT INVESTING ARE

1.

2.

3.

4.

5.

6.

7.

8.

Your hidden treasure...
IS YOUR PASSION!

We all have some! We are born with it inside ourselves.
Well, where is it? Show it to me! How much is it worth?

Your INNER PASSION is your hidden treasure, and it's worth a FORTUNE. All you have to do is bring it out and use it. There is nothing like it – nothing! It comes from the heart, not the wallet.

Let me tell you a story from the days when I ran a wholesale video business. One day a friend said he wanted to see me because he had something important to discuss. He was quite financially successful, and as it turned out, he wanted me to buy his commercial building – and deal with me directly without a real estate agent.

After our meeting he said, "Jim, I see that you are successful in business and perhaps more so than me in many ways. From the moment I stepped into your office, a warm feeling came over me. Your office is different than most – it has unique decor, is very cheerful and without a doubt, it puts you in a good mood! What really captures me is a silence of some kind. I can feel the passion you have for your business without you uttering a single word. It's a warm, secure, satisfying feeling that expresses your passion."

Well, of course I was surprised and thrilled to hear his words. I had just told my sales staff that to be really successful you have to be passionate about what you are doing! If you go to work every day and don't put a whole lot of effort into your job (especially if you are in sales), then your success is just going to be hum drum average. But if you are passionate about what you are doing, I believe people will pick up on it. They will want your warm, caring, inspirational vibe and they will want to deal only with you. Even if you are busy serving someone else they will actually wait to talk with you, even if others are there to help. They will not only want to deal with you but will automatically tell their friends about you…and you'll soon have new clients asking for you by name.

So, where did all these new leads come from? Why are you so lucky, and your fellow workers are not?

Your passion is reflected in everything you do. When you have a passion for something, you enjoy what you are doing immensely. You arrive at work early and usually are the last to leave. It does not matter what else is going on in the world because you are totally focused on pleasing others and in return, you are being rewarded not only financially but also emotionally and socially.
Once you find your passion and start to pull it out from inside you, you will be amazed at all the positive changes that will start to happen in your life. Luck has nothing to do with it – you made it happen and others who do not understand will simply say, "Oh, he's just lucky." You create your own luck.

You create your success!

Passionate people are far and few between. In my life I have only met a few people that I consider to be truly passionate about their life and work, and yes, these people are extremely successful. When you are passionate about your work (and life!) you don't have to run around telling everybody what you are doing – they will start to feel your passion and want to associate with you.

You have to work on developing your passion. It does not happen over night and it will not happen with only a 50% effort. Passion has to be carried through your entire day, week, and year! Your mind has to be focused. Your attitude has to be positive. Your level of passion will be reflected in everything you do – from how you dress for work, how you treat your fellow workers, how you help those in need, what time you show up for work to what time you leave. When you are passionate about life you will help your fellow man without thinking, "what's in it for me". Eventually helping becomes an automatic gesture.

Once you start to feel it, passion becomes part of what you do without thinking about it. That's the true beauty of your hidden treasure. It's huge, it's real, and it's there to share with the rest of the world.

How do you start finding your passion?
Where do you find it?
Where do you start looking for it?
How do you know when you have found it?

Sit in front of your vision board, pull out your humble pebble and

think about

WHAT MOTIVATES YOU.

Is it money?
Sex?
Power?
Clothes?
Shopping?
Helping others?
Pleasing others?
Proving something to someone or yourself?
Is it being the best at what you do?

Be honest because otherwise, you cannot move forward.

EASY MONEY SMARTS
WHAT MOTIVATES ME!

1.

2.

3.

4.

5.

6.

7.

8.

My passion did not start with my job. I was a burn victim when I was three years old and spent almost one year in a hospital – my entire back and bottom was burnt. It was not only a physical scar but also an emotional one – and to this day I never take my shirt off in public. As a young child it was difficult because children can be cruel, but now as an adult I can look at the positive side of the experience – and I believe it made me stronger. Because of my past, I was passionate about connecting with children, so I volunteered at the burn unit of the children's ward at my local hospital. (Needless to say, it was heart-wrenching to be there.)

Do you think for one minute that these children cared if I had a ton of money? NO! They cared because I wanted to help them. I tried putting a smile on their face by donating things like movies or hiring clowns or bringing them donuts to help take their minds off of the suffering just for a short while. It gave them hope and lifted their spirits. Volunteering is a great spiritual cleanser.

Once I started helping these children I started to notice a difference in my life and business. I began to look at things differently – my problems seemed trivial by comparison. Life, I realized, was not just about making money. For me to succeed, I had to help others. And so I did. In return, my business reached heights I could only dream about. Business was so good that I went out on a limb and purchased a commercial building and proceeded to open the first video superstore in southwestern Ontario, Canada.

What did I do to deserve this? I was an average working Joe and did not consider myself a brilliant person on any level. It all came about because I had developed a passion, a true 100% devotion, to help children without expecting anything in return for my efforts.

I was so touched by these children that it brought out something inside of me that at the time I could not understand. I did not have a mentor or coach to guide me. I had no idea my passion could be so powerful. And I certainly had no idea my passion could be so rewarding.

Imagine waking up one day and discovering your business had grown 1000% in volume.

I had not done anything different except I found my treasure inside me.

My passion – to work with sick children.

Don't count on luck to get you there, count on your heart and what you can contribute. Then the reward will come. There is an old saying "if at first you don't succeed try again and again". This is so true! In the beginning you may feel that things are not happening fast enough. The secret is to focus on giving – your passion.

Trust me – the rewards will come.

YOUR PASSION.

Don't live another day without it.
It comes from the heart, not the wallet.
Pass it on!

DAILY HABITS – OPPORTUNITIES TO SAVE

Let's talk about daily habits and how they influence our opportunities for saving. For example, if you smoke and cut out just one cigarette a day, you would save about fifteen dollars a month. It's better for your health, the environment, and definitely your savings account. It is not how much money you make that counts, but how much you save.

I want you to fill out the following list of your good and bad habits so you can see where there are opportunities to save. Be honest. because this book is all about YOU, what's the point in lying to yourself? Write whatever comes to mind. List as many as you want – a few, or a lot – it's entirely up to you.

EASY MONEY SMARTS

MY GOOD HABITS ARE:

1.

2.

3.

4.

5.

EASY MONEY SMARTS

MY NOT SO GOOD HABITS ARE:

1.

2.

3.

4.

5.

That was an honesty test. And I hope you passed with flying colours! Take a good look at your strengths and use them in a positive way to offset your bad habits (or your negative list). For example, if you give up one cigarette a day, you will not really notice it. Here's a tip for substituting a bad addiction with a good one. Pull out your favourite album or CD and play it for ten or fifteen minutes – cranked up a little louder than normal because you really want to enjoy this just as much as that cigarette you would have been smoking. Fifteen minutes later you will be in a positive frame of mind and probably did not even miss that one cigarette! You will have changed a negative action into a positive one, and I'll bet you'll feel great inside and out.

You only need to make small changes in your lifestyle to start seeing opportunities for saving. We have all heard the old saying that humans are creatures of habit. It's true, but we're going to change the bad ones for good ones. Once you start making small change, you'll be amazed at the results – and probably wish you had done this years ago.

PLAN SOME POSITIVE CHANGES

We all could make some changes for the better that wouldn't dramatically interrupt our life style. List three positive changes to get you on the road to saving money and improving your financial situation to date. These changes could really turn your life around.

EASY MONEY SMARTS
3 POSITIVE CHANGES I CAN COMMIT TO *RIGHT* NOW:

1.

2.

3.

THE GOOD HABITS PUZZLE

Let's have some fun with a puzzle designed to help turn old habits into savings.

Here are some examples of negative habits that one could change. Note that there is a time commitment attached to each one.

1. *Cut out one cigarette a day, everyday, for three months.*
2. *Cut out one take-out coffee every week for three months.*
3. *Cut out one beer/drink a week for three months.*
4. *Cut out one shopping trip to any store, each week for three months.*
5. *Cut out buying any electronic/gadget once a month for three months.*
6. *Cut out buying one thing related to your car over the next three months.*
7. *Take my lunch to work one extra day per week, (or cut out ordering take-out food once a month for three months).*

Now, list a few of your negative habits that you are willing to change. Define the time commitment.

EASY MONEY SMARTS

FIVE NEGATIVE HABITS I WILL CHANGE:

1. NEGATIVE HABIT:

TIME COMMITMENT:

2. NEGATIVE HABIT:

TIME COMMITMENT:

3. NEGATIVE HABIT:

TIME COMMITMENT:

4. NEGATIVE HABIT:

TIME COMMITMENT:

5. NEGATIVE HABIT:

TIME COMMITMENT:

THE GOOD HABITS PUZZLE

The goal is to transform this black and white ribbon puzzle into a coloured one. Write down one bad habit in each blank puzzle piece (fill in as many bad habits you want to change). Every time you succeed in changing that behavior, colour that shape. Once you have completed several positive changes, your coloured puzzle will visually show what progress you have made. Even if it takes six months to complete this, it will be worth it.

The GOOD HABITS PUZZLE may seem childish, but it's important to keep motivated and on your path. Colouring in one or two numbered spaces each day may seem trivial, but believe me, it is encouraging. The more things you do for positive reinforcement, the better the chances are of reaching your goals.

If at any time you feel like you can't do these simple tasks, just sit and look at your vision board and take out your humble pebble. Think positive. Positive attitudes and positive emotions are attributes that you need. They will make you successful on the inside and financially successful on the outside.

*Find **happiness first**,*

not money.

From there all good things will follow!

CHAPTER 1 RECAP

WHO ARE YOU?
(REALLY!)

1. Fill our your answers to the questions asked in this chapter. It will help clarify your intentions.

2. Build your vision board. Take your time – it should motivate you in a positive way. Remember this is your dream! This is your goal! Plan it carefully and with respect. You will attract what you desire.

3. Find your humble pebble. Treat it with respect because it represents what is inside of you – your heart and soul – what you are thinking and what you are dreaming. It is your best friend. You can talk to it, you can hold it tight, and you can smile at it. You can tell it your most inner and deepest thoughts. You can yell at it when you are upset or you can just hold it and cherish what it represents. Carry it in your pocket and throughout your day pull it out and reflect on how good things are and what you have to be thankful for. Always be positive.

4. Define your good and not so good habits, then convert your negative habits into lifetime positive habits.

EASY MONEY SMARTS TIP

On a small card, about the size of a business card, write your goals on one side, and things you are grateful for on the other side. Always carry this card with you.

ANADA
50
20

CHAPTER 2

YOU – THE SAVER

SELF WORTH BUILDS NET WORTH!

This chapter is designed to get you thinking about your relationship with money – how you spend it – and how you need it to become good at saving in order to invest.

SAVING MONEY: STEP 1

CHANGE YOUR SPENDING HABITS

Let's start by thinking about ways to cut your monthly expenses. This is about getting back to the basics. Saving money is the first step to financial security. Think of it as your training ground – the skills you need to develop in order to move up to the higher levels of financial success.

Commit to cutting your monthly expenses.

This is a MUST DO.

Little things add up!

Instead of...

...going out for lunch, **bring it from home.**
...buying books, **go to your library** (for movies too).
...driving, **car pool or take public transit**.
...buying new clothes, **update, mend or alter** yours.
...ordering 'another' beer, **make the first one last!**
...going to a movie, **rent a DVD** – shop around for the best deals.

...paying for entertainment, entertain yourself by **reading, walking, playing cards or visiting**.

SCALE BACK.

If you don't really need it, don't buy it, especially major purchases such as a television, car, clothing or DVD's. **Make do with what you have.** You will see a huge jump in your savings.

EASY MONEY SMARTS

7 WAYS I CAN CUT MY MONTHLY EXPENSES:

1.

2.

3.

4.

5.

6.

7.

EASY MONEY SMARTS

79 WAYS YOU CAN SAVE

EATING & DRINKING SAVING TIPS

1. Reduce the coffee shop habit. Make it at home or work.

2. Reduce the fast food habit. Learn to cook and eat at home. Start your day with a good breakfast and bring your lunch.

3. Always make a shopping list and have something to eat before you go grocery shopping. You can think more logically and stick to your list after you have eaten.

4. Check your receipt for accuracy – sometimes scanners are not updated and old higher prices show up.

5. Use coupons for immediate discounts on single items.

6. Buy store generic products. They are usually cheaper than the big brand names and normally the quality is not that different.

7. Use tap water instead of bottled water. Often bottled water is simply tap water! Save your money and help the environment too.

8. Consider brewing your own beer or making your own wine at a fraction of the cost. Make it a club thing where you swap products with your buddies.

9. Buy day old bread.

BANKING & CREDIT CARDS SAVING TIPS

10. Talk with your bank and try and find the cheapest fees for the amount of cheques you write every month. In Canada, President's Choice and ING offers a no fee account. You can save around $20 a month. Put that extra money into your tins (discussed in next chapter).

11. Never use an ATM banking machine – they charge a fee. Instead, go to your own bank's instant teller.

12. Close down your 'shopping cards' (all of your cards that are not Visa, MasterCard or American Express). You will not be tempted to spend unnecessarily and this will also help raise your score over time.

13. Call your remaining credit card companies and ask them to reduce your interest rate. In fact demand it! You will be surprised at your results. *www.cardtrack.com* will help you find credit cards with lower interest rates and better benefits.

INSURANCE SAVING TIPS

14. Insurance companies are not all equal. Shop around and you will find cheaper rates, even if you have a bad record. There is usually a better deal to be found and it could save you hundreds of dollars annually.

15. If you have a Whole Life insurance policy you should cash it out and buy Term insurance. Usually the first three years of your payments on a Whole Life policy goes to sales commissions, fees and bonuses. That gives you less than a zero return on your investment in the early stages. Term insurance will give you the same insurance coverage at a fraction of the cost of Whole Life.

16. Check out *www.insweb.com* and *www.netquote.com* for good insurance rates.

ENERGY SAVING TIPS

17. Rechargeable batteries are a must. There are even some green energy saving ones that hold longer charges and are environmentally friendly at the same time.

18. Hook up your television to a power bar instead of plugging it into the wall. Before you go to bed turn off the power bar. This protects your TV from power surges and lightning and more importantly, it will not suck up hydro while you are sleeping.

19. Your electric stove also sucks hydro. Turn off the breaker when you're not using it.

20. Use energy efficient light bulbs. They will save you money and they last longer.

21. Be more diligent at turning out lights.

22. In summer, set your air conditioner one degree higher, or live with fans instead of using air conditioning.

23. In winter, turn down the heat by one degree (and wear a sweater).

24. Put your Christmas lights on a timer.

25. Cut your water bill by buying a low-flow toilet or place a whole or half a brick in the tank of each toilet to lower its water consumption.

CAR & GASOLINE SAVING TIPS

26. Pay attention to your vehicles maintenance schedules for simple things like oil changes and filters. This will help you get better gas mileage.

27. Instead of buying a new vehicle every three or four years, live with it one year longer.

28. If you lease a vehicle, try to sub lease.

29. Don't idle! Turn the car off.

30. Take local transit, even one day a week, and watch how much gas money you save, not to mention wear and tear on your vehicle. One day a week is 52 days out of the year that you did not drive your car…that's almost 2 months! Big savings in gas alone. This stuff is huge and can fill your savings tins very quickly.

31. If you live in a larger city maybe there are shared automobile plans that are much cheaper to use than owning a car and paying for insurance. *www.zipcar.com / www.autoshare.com*

32. Only buy or fill up your car or truck in the early morning when the ground temperature is still cold. All service stations have their storage tanks buried below ground, and the colder the ground, the more dense the gasoline. When it gets warmer, gasoline expands, so if you're buying gas in the afternoon or in the evening, your gallon is not exactly a gallon. The specific gravity and temperature of the gasoline, diesel, ethanol and other petroleum products plays an important role.

33. When you're filling up do not squeeze the trigger of the nozzle to a fast mode. If you look you will see that the trigger has three (3) stages: low, middle, and high. You should be pumping on low mode, thereby minimizing the vapours that are created while you are pumping. All hoses at the pump have a vapor return. If you are pumping on the fast rate, some of the liquid that goes to your tank becomes vapour, so you're not getting your money's worth.

34. One of the most important tips is to fill up when your gas tank is HALF FULL. The reason for this is the more gas you have in your tank the less air occupying its empty space. Gasoline evaporates faster than you can imagine. Gasoline storage tanks have an internal floating roof. This roof serves as zero clearance between the gas and the atmosphere, so it minimizes the evaporation.

35. Another reminder, if there is a gasoline truck pumping into the storage tanks when you stop to buy gas, DO NOT fill up.Most likely, the gasoline is being stirred up as the gas is being delivered. You might pick up some of the dirt that normally settles on the bottom.

SHOPPING & CELEBRATING

36. If you are shopping for a particular item, ask your friends to watch out for deals, and vice versa. Set up a bargain circle of friends and network your findings by email. Each friend could be asked to follow deals on a certain product so there is no overlapping.

37. For birthday and other presents, reduce your buying by even $5 a gift. Remember it is not how much you spend on someone, it is the fact that you remembered them and are choosing to celebrate with them.

38. Use a calculator to compare prices. Convert items to the same units then compare.

39. Buying in bulk is not always a good idea because you tend to buy more than you need and tie up your cash flow. How many months (or years!) it will take you to use the product?

40. Coupons are not always the best deal when you have to buy certain quantity by a certain time. Is it really a good price? Price check. Sometimes top brand companies will be in a price war with each other and keep offering more discounts to be ahead of their competition. This is where you can score big – just don't over buy! The buy one, get one free, deal on things you don't need is not a good deal.

42. Our family started a fun gift practice every Christmas that provides a lot of entertainment. Everyone wraps and brings a present – an object from home. Everyone draws a number, The person who drew number one picks any present they want and opens it in front of everyone. Person number two can take away the first person's gift or open new present. Number three person can take either the first or second person gift or open a new present. This continues until the last gift is opened…so lots of trading goes on.

43. Make your own gifts. Do you bake? Make jam? Take photos? Home made gifts are excellent way to save money and show love and thoughtfulness. One year, a family friend gave me a knitted 6-foot scarf. It is one of my most favorite gifts because I know it took many hours to make – it came from the heart and was beautiful! I have always thought that the best thing you can give someone as a gift is yourself. Offer a service – wash windows, cut grass, baby-sit, wash and wax a car, or shovel snow.

44. Sell your unwanted or unused things on *www.craiglist.com* – it's free and local.

45. FREE STUFF!
www.giveusfreestuff.com
www.free-samples.ca
www.actualfreestuff.com

SAVING TIPS FOR THE HOME

46. Use your local library for books, and for magazines, movies and free computer time too. Most libraries carry the local newspaper so cancel your home subscription or read it online.

47. Do you really need all those extra high-speed computer connections? Try and reduce your monthly bill by even a few dollars without disrupting your normal online activity.

48. Telephone services are very costly, so try to reduce your monthly phone bill even by a few dollars. If you get the right cell phone plan you might not even need a landline – this could mean one less bill coming in every month. Usually better deals are had by signing a three year contract.

49. Want to get free furniture? As an apartment building owner I discovered that many tenants leave furniture behind. Meet the property manager or superintendent of an apartment unit and offer to clean units as they become vacant. Keep all of the furniture left behind – repair if necessary, clean, and then sell it.

50. Have a "family money meeting" once a month and show a budget for income and expenses. Each month see where you are over-spending or need to cut… and talk about it. Always discuss your goals. Why are we doing this? Where are we going? How quick can we get there? Stay focused on your financial goals – getting out of debt and learning how to save.

51. If you are an apartment owner you can charge more rent if you supply the furniture with the apartment.

52. Colour and cut your own hair – or have a friend or family member do it instead of paying top prices at a salon. Or get your hair styled at a hairdressing school *(for example, www.aveda.com).*

EXTRA CASH SAVING TIPS

53. Start your own part-time business from home. You don't need much to get started on these small business ventures. Network everywhere by putting up notices in variety stores, laundromats, grocery stores, coffee clubs, hair salons and on the internet.
Here are a few ideas:
Dog walking service
Errand runner or delivery person (especially for the elderly)
Driver - if you have a valid drivers license (use their car)
Computer consulting
Cut grass (use their mower)
Shovel snow
Wash windows
Clean out eaves troughs
House painting
Handy man chores
Laundry services
House cleaning services

54. Bartending and waiting on tables provides immediate cash from tips.

55. Babysitting pays instant cash. Drop off notices or knock on doors of people you know who have children. Make sure you have good references.

56. Hold a Saturday car wash. Make your own signs and post your notice in your local paper the day before.

57. Host a yard/garage sale twice a year. Sell some older items that you have stored away and never use any more. You could put these items for sale on *www.ebay.com* to reach a larger audience.

58. Sell scrap metal. Take it to the local salvage yard for immediate cash.

59. Take in a boarder, even if only temporary, to help share living expenses. Sign a short term lease. Ask for first and last month's rent up front for immediate cash.

60. At the end of the day put all your loose change in a savings jar. You won't even miss it and it adds up!

61. Consider selling your old gold jewellery for cash. Many jewellery stores will buy it, but check newspapers and the internet for best rates. *www.webuygold.com*

62. Get paid for your contacts. Do you have any information or contacts that you could sell for a finder's fees to mortgage brokers, real estate agents, financial planners etc.? This is legal as you are supplying them with a qualified lead, which means they will get a commission and can legally pay you a finder's fee. (Normally you would get paid when the deal closes.)

63. Set up a limited company with your accountant or lawyer. By doing this you will be able to legally start paying company related expenses with pre-tax dollars, and this is huge. The expenses come out before you pay tax. This must be a legitimate running company.

64. If you have your finances in reasonable order, put 10% of every dollar that comes into your home into a savings jar. Make this a habit forever. It really boosts up your savings and gets you ready for investing. (More about this in the next chapter.)

65. Don't buy souvenirs – they usually end up as dust collectors. Buy postcards or take pictures instead.

66. Trade in or swap those old DVD movies or books you have just sitting on the shelf. Visit *www.swaptree.com, www.bookmooch.com* or *www.paperbackswap.com.*

67. If you have a dog why buy expensive rawhide treats when you could get beef shin bones from a butcher? They might cost as little as a buck!

68. Read classic books online for free at *www.gutenberg.org.* There are more than 20,000 books to download.
69. If you have unused gift cards lying around – sell or swap them at *www.plasticjungle.com.* You can also buy discounted gift cards here.

70. Avoid dumping charges and recycle things like toys, furniture, appliances and tons of things in between on websites like *www.freecycle.org.* Members at this site list items they want to give away. Also see *www.freesharing.org* or *www.sharingisgiving.org.*

71. Learn how to get a good hotel discount simply by asking the right questions. Here is one example using a Sheraton hotel, found on *www.priceline.ca*, where the best available rate was listed at $209.

1. We asked if there are any club discounts (like an auto club) and the price was reduced to $170

2. We then asked for a non-refundable rate, which reduced the room to $150
3. We then asked if they had a limited time offer and once again the price was dropped to $130.

72. Why pay for big brand names when it comes to laundry soap? Simply use an inexpensive bar of soap and a cheese grater and fill 1/3 of a cup per wash load.

73. Want immediate cash? Take something of value that you have not used in a long time to your local pawn shop...things like DVDs, instruments or jewellery. They will normally give you around 10% of its value, which is about the same as you would get at a garage sale except you get cash instantly. If you have second thoughts about selling an item, you normally have 90+ days to go back and recoup it for a small fee.

74. Why buy expensive pest controls for your garden? Fill a trigger sprayer with liquid soap and water. You will need to spray every day for about a week and if it rains you need to start all over again. This works well on some (but not all) insects.

75. Try this web site to find out how to save on your long distance calls within Canada or to the United States: *www.magicjacks.ca.* These 'magic jacks' are plugged into your computer then into your phone. (Presently they don't work for cell phones, but I am sure it won't be long.)

76. *www.fatwallet.com* features coupons, lots of savings, and even rebate information.

77. Download the app at *www.shoppinggenie.com* for the best price comparisons on big ticket items. (Windows only)

78. Having a tough time keeping up payments for expensive medications, especially if you are not on a plan? Try *www.needymeds.org*, a discount prescription drug clearing house. You still need to submit your doctors prescription. This is a legitimate service and you'll need to follow government rules and regulations, but it could save you money. In Ontario, use the Trillium Drug plan. The quarterly deductible is based on your revenue, and thereafter each prescription is only $2.00. For other provinces, check with your pharmacist.

79. Check out *www.hotwire.ca* or *www.redflagdeals.com* for last minutes hotel deals. Don't forget to ask about additional charges – is parking included? Are tips and any gratuities already added?

THE CREDIT CARD GAME

CREDIT CARDS

Credit cards are an awesome tool for emergencies, travelling or business expenses, but unfortunately most people use them to buy stuff they could live without. Did you know, however, that you can call credit card companies to request a reduction in interest charges, and increase your credit limit? Do not be afraid to ask to speak with a supervisor if the agent on the phone is uncooperative. Don't be afraid to tell them that you are thinking of switching credit card companies. The increase in the limit is good for your credit rating but do not under any circumstance spend it. I repeat never, NEVER spend it. The higher the credit limit on your cards means your current balance is much less than your maximum – this is good for your credit score. Just keep it that way! Keep phoning every six months to ask for these things.

CARDS WITH ANNUAL FEES

Normally credit cards with no fees have a higher interest rate and cards with fees have lower interest rates. On credit cards where you do not carry a balance, use the higher interest/no fee card because it is not costing you anything. On the other hand, if you are carrying a balance, use the one with a fee/lower interest rate. Always take the fees into account when you check your balances and charges. Divide them by 12 and include them in your monthly statement to calculate exactly just how much you are paying on your debt each month. It should be considerably lower than any high interest card. Or else you are getting a bad deal and you should call and complain to your credit card company.

TRANSFERING CREDIT CARD BALANCES

Transfer any credit card balance to another card offering a lower interest rate, even if it's just for a short time. Keep it there for as long as you can to get the maximum benefit. But keep an eye on the date the offer expires.

AIR MILES AND OTHER REWARD PROGRAMS

These are good as long as you're buying something you need. If you're just spending to accumulate points or air miles, you might as well just go out and buy the item you want because it will be cheaper than accumulating points.

Loyalty programs are marketing tools to get you to spend more at your favourite stores, but they may cost you more in the end. It may make you feel good to be rewarded for buying, but check to see if the item you're interested in is at its lowest price. Don't be conned into overspending.

YOUR CREDIT RATING

Credit scores and understanding them is extremely important in life. Credit bureau scores are based on information maintained at the credit reporting agencies. The most widely used credit scores are known as FICO scores.

If you have had a poor credit history it can be corrected but it does take time. As recent good payment patterns show up, your score will go up accordingly. Do not let a bad credit score bring you down.

Lenders who use the credit scoring system get precise information about you on which to base credit decisions. Most lenders have their own guidelines, so if one lender turns you down a different lender may approve you.

Your credit report gives details about your credit history as it has been reported to the credit reporting agencies by your current lenders. Your report shows what types of credit you use, how long your accounts has been open, and if you have paid your bills on time. It will show any public records or collection items. This information comes from the courts and collection agencies plus public record information on bankruptcies, foreclosures, lawsuits, wage garnishment, liens or judgments.

Credit reports give lenders an overall view of your credit history. They let lenders know how much credit you have used and if you are seeking out new sources for credit. It will show what inquiries you have initiated to get new loans. It will show the date, name of the company, and how much you were requesting.

Your credit report will also show what is referred to as your trade lines or companies you owe money to, when you got the loan, how much money was originally given to you, your current balance, and your history of paying or delinquency.

If you do not have a credit score it will be difficult for you to get a mortgage or a new car if you will require financing. Without a credit score or record it will be almost impossible to get a loan.

The 3 credit reporting agencies are:
1. Equifax – their FICO score is called a Beacon score.
2. Experian – their FICO score is called Experian/Fair, Isaac risk model.
3. Trans Union – their FICO score is called Empirica.

Your score may be different at all three reporting agencies. The best advice here is to manage your credit very responsibly over time. Closing an account where you had missed a payment or two will not make that item disappear from your credit report. If you have missed payments then get yourself current and stay current.

TIPS FOR RAISING YOUR CREDIT SCORE

1. Pay your bills on time. ALWAYS.

2. Keep credit card balances low, or at zero.

3. Use strategies to get rid of debt by incorporating all the saving tips found in this book.

4. If you are having trouble making ends meet then contact your creditors and redo loan amounts and payment schedules.

5. If you just started to get a credit score do not open a lot of new accounts too fast.

6. Apply for, and only open credit card accounts as needed.

7. Get rid of all your 'shopping cards' because they bring down your credit score.

The only credit cards you need are the three big ones. One card for VISA, one for MasterCard, and one for American Express. No other cards should be in your possession as they work against your credit because they are classified as strictly shopping cards. The three big cards are good for emergencies, which we all get. But pay off the balances as they become due. Owing a lot of money on many accounts can indicate that you are overextended and are at risk of missing payments, or not being able to make them at all.

You are also entitled to a free copy of your credit report within a 60-day period, which you can request from credit agencies. It will not affect your credit score if you request your own credit report. Also, any request for a pre-approval will not affect your score.

Applications for credit will remain on your credit score for two years. One or two inquiries will not affect your score. However, a lot of inquiries, like ten or more, will have a huge impact on your credit score because now it is obvious that you are desperate or in serious trouble. All inquiries are listed on your score and when a lending institution sees that you have been looking all over town they get nervous and will automatically decline you.

If you are turned down for new credit the Equal Credit Opportunity Act (ECOA) gives you the right to obtain the reasons why you were turned down.

You should check your credit report to make sure all the information in your report is correct. If you find an error in your credit report the agencies must investigate and respond to you within 30 days.

How to contact these credit-reporting agencies:
1. Equifax: (800) 685-1111 or *www.equifax.com*
2. Experian: (888) 397-3742 or *www.experian.com*
3. Trans Union: (800) 916-8800 or www.transunion.com

GOVERNMENT SAVING INITIATIVES

GOVERNMENT BONDS

A good savings vehicle is Government Bonds, especially through your job's payroll deduction plan where a few dollars is taken off your paycheck and put into a saving fund until you have enough saved up to purchase the Bond. This saving plan is really good for people who have difficulty saving because the few dollars taken off each pay cheque is not missed. While bonds do not pay high interest, the whole point is that you are being forced to save and that's great.

$5,000 TAX FREE SAVINGS ACCOUNT

This is a great investing tool and everybody should be taking advantage of it. You can invest up to $5,000 a year, and never pay tax on your investment returns. Any unused amounts can be contributed in future years. You can withdraw your money at anytime, tax free.

You must be a Canadian resident and over 18 years of age with a SIN number. Money can be gifted by a parent, grandparent, or spouse.

Withdrawls are not considered income and are not taxable and do not impact your Child Tax Benefit, Old Age Security, or any Guaranteed Income Supplement.

At the time of this writing, there are three types of investments allowed in this program:
1. Straight cash to sit in your account and earn interest
2. Mutual funds and corporate shares
3. Guaranteed Investment Certificates – GIC's

Note that all of these must be done through your local bank.

SAVING MONEY: STEP 2
RECORD YOUR PERSONAL BUDGET

Once you begin to honestly record your income and expenses each month, you'll get a clear picture of your financial situation. It will be easy to see where your money is actually going and where you can cut some expenses. Soon you'll be able to see your expenses going down and your saving and investment contributions going up.

Before you fill in the amounts, you may want to put your vision board in front of you and get in touch with your humble pebble.

Write your figures in pencil so you can erase if you make a mistake. Be as accurate and as realistic as possible. Put down the true figures. This is the only way you can monitor how well this will work. There is no reason to be embarrassed about your numbers. This is your life and you are doing something positive.

Get the hang of filling out these monthly financial statements – just like all the big companies. These figures tell a story – YOUR financial story about where you started and how you are growing – how healthy you are financially.

PART A

YOUR INCOME & EXPENSES

MONTH:

EARNED INCOME (MONTHLY)

Job full time	$
Job part time	$
Pension	$
Other	$
SUB-TOTAL	**$**

INVESTMENT INCOME

Real estate	$
Self employment	$
SUB-TOTAL	**$**

PORTFOLIO INCOME

Stocks	$
Bonds	$
Interest	$
Other	$
SUB-TOTAL	**$**

***TOTAL INCOME: $

EXPENSES (MONTHLY)

Home mortgage	$
Rent	$
Car Payment	$
2nd Car Payment	$
Food	$
Heating	$
Clothing	$
Internet/Cable	$
Phone	$
Hydro	$
Car Insurance	$
Car Maintenance	$
Home Insurance	$
Medications	$
Gifts, treats	$
Other	$

***** TOTAL MONTHLY EXPENSES: $**

*****NET MONTHLY CASH FLOW: $**

(The difference between your income and expenses)

The net monthly cash flow is the ***most important figure.***

It will tell you exactly how much surplus money you have at the end

of each month – or if you are short. If the latter, you need to do one of two things:
a) increase your monthly income or
b) cut your expenses.

PART B

YOUR ASSETS & LIABILITES

MONTH:

ASSETS

Bank account-chequing	$
Bank account-savings	$
House	$
Investment property	$
Car	$
2nd Vehicle	$
Valuable possessions	$
Stocks	$
Bonds	$
Receivables	$
Other investments	$

*****TOTAL ASSETS: $**

LIABILITIES

Mortgage	$
Car loans	$
Credit cards	$
Personal loans	$
Investment loans	$
Business loans	$
Stocks	$
Life Insurance policies	$
Other debts	$

*****TOTAL LIABILITIES: $**

SAVING MONEY: STEP 3
THE FOUR JARS

DEBT, INVEST, CHARITY, SPLURGE

This is one saving and investing investment tool that I really like because it's simple and effective. But the principles are the same as larger projects, just on a much smaller scale. I use 4 canisters – they can be jugs or bottles – just make sure that you cannot see through them. (It's less tempting to spend if you can't see money, so make sure they are a solid colour.) Two canisters should be large and two should be small. Label the large canisters DEBT and INVESTING and label the small ones CHARITY and SPLURGE.

Decide what you can afford and every week put money in each canister. Pick an amount that you are comfortable with and stick to it every week. Some people are just plain and simply terrible at saving money but they can really help themselves with this small saving tool.

Something like this example:

$2 for debt
$2 for investing
$1 for charity
$1 for splurges

$6 weekly from loose change

Place the 4 containers on the same table as your vision board so you will be encouraged to save.

When you get enough money built up in your DEBT jar, pay off your high interest debt as soon as possible. This investment tool is designed to help you save and make saving a regular habit.

The next jar labelled INVESTING is for just that. Put the money into whatever investment you wish. You may want to pick one investment so you have a goal in mind. I originally started putting $10 a week in my investment jar and got so excited I increased it to $20 because I wanted to buy shares in Google· and the $10 weekly fix just was not getting me there quickly enough. I was truly motivated and had my jars on the table next to my vision board.

One of the smaller jars marked CHARITY is very fulfilling because this allows you to decide what charity you want to donate to, or get involved in. You could buy tickets on a hospital lottery where you could win a car or a dream home and the money goes to support the hospital. This adds a little excitement! You could also buy toys at Christmas and donate them to the children's hospital. It's a good feeling helping less fortunate children at the most wonderful time of the year.

Your other small jar labelled SPLURGE is just what it says – go ahead and buy that little thing. Treat yourself for doing a great job of following your dreams and goals through savings.

You need to learn to save before you learn to invest. Just like learning to walk before you learn to run. You need to establish good saving habits and stick with them. This is no small feat – a lot of people have no saving habits at all. Their intensions may be good but they never get ahead because either they procrastinate or they are shopaholics and just cannot seem to hold on to a dollar. Remember the old expression "money seems to burn a hole in their pocket".

SAVING MONEY: STEP 4

BUILD YOUR TEAM OF EXPERTS

SURROUND YOURSELF WITH A TEAM OF PROFESSIONALS. People who are loyal and dedicated, just like you.

Look for a lawyer specializing in real estate, along with a licensed real estate person, an insurance broker, a licensed creative mortgage broker, and an accountant (also experienced in real estate). Set a time frame when you will talk to them. Relay this: You have just read Jim Mathe's Easy Money Smarts and are starting to put money aside. In the near future you will be needing their services. You are not wealthy YET, but will be consistent with your savings and are dedicated to being more successful.

MY TEAM OF EXPERTS

LAWYER
contact info

REAL ESTATE AGENT
contact info

MORTGAGE BROKER
contact info

ACCOUNTANT
contact info

INSURANCE BROKER
contact info

SAVING MONEY: STEP 5

BUILD YOUR SKILL SET

To be successful you have to be informed.

Maybe you don't understand the extra costs incurred when buying a house? Or tax laws related to inheritance? What skills do you not have, but will need, in order to reach your financial goals?

Attend seminars about real estate, tax tips, creative mortgaging, life insurance, and financial planning…and attend my Easy Money Smarts seminars! *(www.easymoneysmarts.com)* Take your spouse or a close friend if they are as positive as you!

WHAT SKILLS DO I STILL NEED TO BECOME FINANCIALLY SUCCESSFUL? WHERE CAN I FIND THEM?

1.

2.

3.

4.

5.

SAVING MONEY: STEP 6
THINK AND ACT SUCCESSFULLY

BECOME FINANCIALLY LITERATE.

Use the correct terms when talking to your banker, accountant, real estate broker, mortgage specialist, lawyer, stockbroker or financial planner. Read and reread the financial terms listed in the back of this book.

WORD OF ADVICE

Don't be afraid to read this chapter, or this entire book, a second or third time. You need to fully understand the basics until they become a routine in your life. Cutting expenses so you have money to start saving, developing your plan of where you want to go and how you want to live. And finally, have some investments working for you.

CHAPTER 2 RECAP
YOU – THE SAVER

1. How can you cut your monthly expenses? List the things you really could live without and stick with it. If you don't need it, don't buy it – needs and wants are two different things. Find creative ways to save!

2. Record your personal budget. A monthly budget of your income and expenses will give you a good understanding of how much money is coming in and going out.

3. Handle your credit cards wisely, understand your credit score and build a strong credit rating.

4. Set up your 4 jars: debt, invest, charity and splurge. Always allow a spot in expenses for investments no matter how small the amount. As long as you are diligently putting money away every month to invest, investing will soon become a habit.

5. Build your team of experts.

6. Define what skills you still need to acquire to be financially successful.

7. Become financially literate. Review the terminology at the end of this book.

"We make a living by what we get and a life by what we give."

Sir Winston Churchill

CHAPTER THREE

YOU – THE INVESTOR PART 1

JOINT VENTURES IN REAL ESTATE

A joint venture is the ideal way to get into real estate without investing any money especially if you don't have any money.
It's perfect!

ABOUT JOINT VENTURES IN REAL ESTATE

In joint ventures, two parties form a partnership with each performing clearly outlined tasks. One partner puts up all the money (usually busy, high income earners looking for a return on their investment) while the second partner (you!) performs all the work – picking the property, budgeting it, renting it out, managing it, and finally selling it.

The profit is normally split 50/50.

This is the beauty of joint ventures. You don't need any money!

An agreement is usually signed in advance before anything is started, because there are always risks involved in any real estate deal. The contract will outline each partner's responsibilities, what the split of money is when the property is sold, and what happens if the project goes sour.

Joint ventures are great when the two parties can work well together and fully trust and respect the partnership. They will not work if one party tries to take over or treat the other party unfairly. Joint ventures are normally not long term agreements, but if you work well together and make tons of money why not keep going? It's important to be extremely honest and integral, committed 100% to your partner and the project. If a project is over budget and looses money, then the money partner will not be happy because they have lost their investment. And you won't be happy because you will not be paid for your time and your reputation will be harmed for future deals. Even if it was not your fault, you are the one in charge and that's all that matters to investors.

The money partner is basically investing in the partner (you) who is putting the deal together. It all comes down to you, how well you did, and how well you communicated with your joint venture partner. I cannot stress integrity enough. Remember, your deal has to be genuine. If you would not invest money in the idea, why would you ask someone else to?

The investor puts up all the money for the deal including closing costs, but not a penny more. If you go over budget it is your problem, not the investors. You will have to come up with the needed extra money because you made the mistake of under budgeting. You can never go back to the investor for more money (never!) once the deal has been struck. Let's say you made a $1,800 over budget expense mistake, even if it wasn't your fault, the integrity issue kicks in and you will have to absorb that expense out of your half of the profits.

FINDING YOUR JOINT VENTURE PARTNER

Finding a joint venture partner is not as difficult as you might think. Never go after people with money – let them come to you. Talk about real estate wherever you go, without being pushy or earnest. Those that are interested will inquire and those that are not will not usually participate in the conversation. You will, at least, have planted the seed to all those who heard your conversation. The more people you talk to, the better your odds will be for finding a joint venture partner.

The most important thing is to build a good relationship with your joint venture partner, because when your first project is finished and successful, you will want to use them again for your next project. If you did a good job and both of you made a lot of money, your partner will of course want to team up with you again. Your track record is crucial to your success.

Finding the right project to promote is up to you. Sometimes it might take two or three years to come to fruition. Remember it is your vision, hard work, and management that will turn a certain property around and show a profit.

Because the profit is (usually) equally split, investors need a higher return than the going interest rate. If the going interest rate is low, for example 4%, a joint venture partner will not bother unless they can make around 20% on their money. There is risk involved and they want to be compensated for that – and so they should. If you do not get them a decent return they will not partner with you to do another deal. If mortgage rates are 4%, the banks will be offering even lower rates on savings accounts, possibly ½ of 1%, so there will be lots of potential joint venture prospects.

Don't forget that if the money partner is making a 20% return on their money, you are making 100% because you have no money invested at all. The only risk you have is your time and reputation. In any real estate deal there is always risk and that is why the returns are normally much higher than the conventional rate, but the risk is somewhat reduced because of the asset of real estate.

Have a web site set up for contact purposes perhaps outlining your project(s) and your skills.

To be really successful at joint ventures and finding good partners, you need to network yourself on a weekly basis.
Hand out business cards outlining what you are doing and looking for.
Place a small and direct newspaper ad: "looking for a joint venture partner".
Go to meetings where you can interact with possible clients. Talk to everyone about your real estate opportunities.
Surf the internet.
Place flyers in grocery stores and on community billboards.

PITCHING YOUR IDEA

Remember, the investor is investing in YOU – not the project itself – and if they already know you, all you need to do is layout the deal. That's it. Present your idea and let the deal sell itself.

Don't be afraid to work deals with close friends or relatives, since they know your character make-up. If you have integrity and are reliable and honest, this is a great place to start. Put your plan together, demonstrate your diligence, and show positive realistic outcomes. Don't overstate your profit potential. Investors don't like surprises and it could jeopardize your next deal.

Remember when you talk to prospective clients, even if they are friends or family, always dress appropriately. You must instill confidence. Act and look like a professional with a plan. You want your prospective partner(s) to believe you can do this – that you are the right person for the job. Make them they feel good about working with you. Get character references from your banker, accountant, family doctor or dentist to show prospective joint venture partners.

Make your presentation professional – not long or boring. Get right to the facts and present the outline of your project in about 3 minutes. Practice your presentation at home with your spouse, friend, or in front of a mirror.

Always have your lawyer write up the joint venture agreement and keep it simple. The cost of the lawyer and agreement is part of the cost of the deal and will be at no cost to you. Your mentor *(see Chapter 9)* can supply you with joint venture information to help keep your costs down.

One very important thing! Once you get a commitment from a partner, get him or her to sign a pre-agreement form detailing the amount of money and it's availability date. Will it be available in cash on the closing date? All money goes to your lawyer on the set up, and close down, of a joint venture. The money never touches your hands – and that is a selling feature when you are trying to close a deal: "Your money goes through our lawyer so you do not need to worry that I will run away with your money."

Make sure you have independent lawyers representing each of you separately. This is a must!

Don't be afraid to use articles from newspapers or magazines that discuss growth in real estate close to where you want to invest. Cut out these articles and use them in your presentation. They will help boost confidence in you, your project, and help sell your deal!

If you are not working and need to have an income over part of the project time, you can work that into the cost of the project – your lawyer advancing you funds at certain stages. This will not affect the total outcome of your profit because you factored in these payroll figures, and your partner will know how you are to be advanced this money. However, if you are off target or behind schedule, then your advance will be too.

Set up a joint bank account for each individual project. If you are collecting rents, paying insurance and a mortgage, you will need a chequing account. Have a separate bank account for each project and close it after the project is finished.

Don't be afraid to ask for a safety net of cash in your proposal. When you have purchased the property and paid out all the closing costs, you will still need to get insurance on the property and have money available for repairs and maintenance. It is always nice to have a few thousand dollars for back up.

Any excess cash from the monthly income of the building is split as per your joint venture agreement, which is usually 50/50, and paid when both parties agree to receive it – or it can accumulate and be split when the building is sold.

COMMON QUESTIONS TO ASK YOUR INVESTOR

What do joint venture investors want from the project? You need to know what they are looking for before going into a deal. The following are typical questions you should ask.

What kind of return are you looking for?

How quickly do you want to see those kinds of returns?

How often do you want to see financial statements on this project? (Usually every 3 months is normal)

Do you have other investments now?

How much money could you invest in one deal?

How much money do you want to invest in this deal?

Are these funds available now or is there a specific date that they would be available?

Are your funds coming from a credit card or loan of any kind? (This would add stress on the deal and could hinder the outcome if you had to sell earlier than planned). If the investor does not really HAVE the cash, but instead borrows or raises it, this partnership could be risky. Because he or she is borrowing the cash there is more of a probability of something going wrong – for example, creditors or banks could force the sale of the house you're working on.

Have you ever done a real estate joint venture deal before?

Would you be interested in doing more than one joint venture deal with me at the same time?

On completion of the project, would you be interested in reinvesting part or all of your profits in another project with me?

Is your spouse involved in the decision making?

Give me your honest opinion/feedback on this project and any changes you would like to see made before we go to our independent lawyers.

When is the best time to contact you?

What is the best way to contact you?

When can I get a letter of intent from you or your lawyer so I know you are serious to start the deal?

Can we set a date to see our lawyers to get the deal in progress?

Can we set a time to visit a bank to open an account?

Do you have friends, relatives, or know somebody who might be interested in working on a joint venture deal with me?

YOUR INFO KIT

Presenting an information kit to prospective partners makes you appear professional and confident. Never mail these out – if someone wants one, they have to meet you in person. Personal contact is huge so don't give it away. Use the following guidelines to build your content.

1. Introduction page with your name, credentials, and any previous projects that you have worked on.

2. A colour photo and description of the property.

3. Your plan – what you intend to do with the property.

4. A financial statement outlining all the costs, income, and profit potential.

5. Any other information about the area or city that would help increase confidence – from newspapers, magazines, or online.

6. Your professional business card. Complete with your name, address, and contact information – phone, cell or email.

TIPS FOR NEGOTIATING YOUR DEAL

Always have an exit strategy written in the contract. If it doesn't work according to plan, how are you going to get out of the deal – without having to pay a penalty or losing your deposit?

Every joint venture partnership is different, just like the partners. So every agreement may vary from partner to partner and deal to deal. For example, both names might secure the mortgage equally, or if your credit is weak, then the investing partner may agree to secure it alone, in return for an additional 5+%. It will be up to you to negotiate with each partner, on each deal.

It doesn't matter if only one person is registered on title or on the mortgage. You are fully protected as long as your lawyer has an enforceable joint venture agreement registered at the same time.

If one party wants to sell the property, the other party has the first right of refusal. Normally an accredited appraisal is done on the property and that is the value that is used to divide money between parties if one partner is selling out.

Always have an accountant do your joint venture statements and taxes. This way, there is no misunderstanding and you can be advised on tax advantages and possible loopholes. This eliminates surprises and keeps everyone honest.

Never guarantee a return figure. Ever! A joint venture has risks. Keep your projections modest, because it's better to receive a bigger cheque on closing than you forecasted. If the return is better than you predicted, you'll look like a hero.

Each joint venture deal you do can have a different strategy. For example, some partners may be looking for short term deals only. Another partner may be looking for a medium to long term deal where you keep a property for a 5 to 7 year term. You need to work with each joint venture partner to satisfy both of your goals. This is why it is a good idea to have several joint venture partners.

A mentor *(see Chapter 9)* can be a big help if you're looking for a joint venture partner.

Never get too emotional over a deal – business is business and it's best to leave your emotional side at home as it may warp your sense of judgment.

Always trust your gut feeling. If you get a bad vibe or something feels wrong, walk away from the deal.

It's not how good you are, it's how hard you are willing to work to succeed.

FYI: An interesting real estate deal site is www.landauction.com.

CHAPTER FOUR

YOU – THE INVESTOR PART 2

BUYING A SECOND PROPERTY

THE INVESTMENT OF A LIFETIME!

INVESTING IN REAL ESTATE

History has shown that in the long run real estate is one of the most solid investments. It is a hedge against inflation with the potential of bringing real wealth to the investor. Because real estate is long term, the longer you wait the longer it is going to take you to reap the rewards. The longer it takes you to get in the game the more money you are loosing.

The population of the world is increasing dramatically. This puts stress on the real estate market driving prices up, creating opportunities for investors. Remember there is only so much land available, especially in good areas, and once it's gone it's gone, and so will today's prices.

Real estate is probably the easiest way to build wealth and no doubt the safest as long as you use professional help.

Over time, owning a second house will make you rich.

It's the all-time, no-brainer investment.

And your retirement will be a lot easier because you will have cash from selling your second house.

BUYING A SECOND PROPERTY – THE INVESTMENT OF A LIFETIME

I recommend that you buy a simple three-bedroom home in a nice part of town. Be sure it's all fixed up and ready to rent out. Get first and last months rent up front, have tenants sign a lease, and ask for references. Speak to their previous landlord to see if there were any problems. Yes, there will be headaches along the way but nothing the average person can't deal with.

Always inspect a property yourself before you buy. Take your time and don't be afraid to be critical – it's your investment and future.

Never purchase any property without a home inspection by a professional qualified home inspector. Ask them for references, how long have they been doing this, and if they guarantee their work.

So, take this nice starter home (let's say you pay $295,000), and put 20% down ($59,000) according to new government regulations. You'll carry a $236,000 mortgage @ 3.89% interest over a 5 year term with a 25 year amortization (and yes, the rates will vary over the remaining 20 years of mortgage).

Your monthly payment would be $1,227.37 plus insurance, property taxes, property insurance, and liability for a total of $1500 per month. To cover all your costs and make a profit you'll need to rent out this home for $1700 a month.

When you rent out your income property you get first and last months rent up front. On day one you have a cheque for $3,400 (first and last) and you're earning a profit of $200 per month. You may want to offer a bonus back to the tenant if they pay their rent on time and look after all minor repairs without bothering you. (However, you will definitely want them to call you if something major goes wrong. Giving something like a $100 per month rebate could save you a lot of headaches and time with silly little things.)

Now that the house is rented, all you have to do is take your profit to the bank. At this point, I highly recommend that you DO NOT SPEND this extra cash. Reinvest it and do the same with the interest.

You will be amazed at how quickly it will accumulate and how much cash you will have.

In the next few pages, I've calculated what would happen if you diligently save this money over the next twenty five years.

NOTE: ALL FIGURES ARE APPROXIMATE VALUES INCLUDING TAXES

YEAR 1
First and last month's rent $3,400
The monthly profit for one year is approximately $2,400
Put this directly into a RRSP to defer paying tax on it.

NOTE: You can only claim the interest portion of your mortgage payment as an expense and will have to pay tax on principal amount being paid monthly unless you depreciate it over the term of mortgage. If you sell the property, this deferred tax has to be paid back – but at least it does not have to come out of your pocket directly each month and has no interest – so why not use that to your advantage!

Estimated 5% interest for one year ($3,400 + $2,400 = $5,800) is $202
Put this year's profit ($2,400 + $202) into a RRSP.
At the end of the first year you have $6,002 in cash!

YEAR 2
At the start of the second year you have a rent increase of 1.5%, $25.50 monthly (but the increase may be offset by higher expenses, so no real gain)

At the start of the second year you have $6,002
Second year rental profit $2,400
Estimated 5% interest for one year $364
Put this year's profit into a RRSP.
At the end of the second year you have $8,766 in cash!

YEAR 3
At the start of the third year you have $8,766
Third year rental profit $2,400
Estimated 5% interest for one year $502
Put this year's profit into a RRSP.
At the end of the third year you have $11,668 in cash!

YEAR 4
At the start of the fourth year you have $11,668
Fourth year rental profit $2,400
Estimated 5% interest for one year $647
Put this year's profit into a RRSP.
End of the fourth year you have $14,715 in cash!

YEAR 5
At the start of the fifth year you have $14,715
Fifth year rental profit $2,400
Estimated 5% interest for one year $800
Put this year's profit into a RRSP.
At the end of the fifth year you have $17,915 in cash!

YEAR 6
At the start of the sixth year you have $17,915
Sixth year rental profit $2,400
Estimated 5% interest for one year $960
Put this year's profit into a RRSP.
At the end of the sixth year you have $21,275 in cash!

YEAR 7
At the start of the seventh year you have $21,275
Seventh year rental profit $2,400
Estimated 5% interest for one year $1,127
Put this year's profit into a RRSP.
At the end of the seventh year you have $24,802 in cash!

This may seem a bit boring because these are just numbers to you, but it is important to see the numbers especially at the end. If you decided to sell at any given point, you would be able to see exactly how much money you should have.

YEAR 8
At the start of the eighth year you have $24,802
Eighth year rental profit $2,400
Estimated 5% interest for one year $1,240
Put this year's profit into a RRSP.
At the end of the eighth year you have $28,442 in cash!

YEAR 9
At the start of the ninth year you have $28,442
Ninth year rental profit $2,400
Estimated 5% interest for one year $1,412
Put this year's profit into a RRSP.
At the end of the ninth year you have $32,264 in cash!

YEAR 10
At the start of the tenth year you have $32,264
Tenth year rental profit $2,400
Estimated 5% interest for one year $1,677
Put this year's profit into a RRSP.
At the end of the tenth year you have $36,341 in cash!

YEAR 11

At the start of the eleventh year you have $36,341
Eleventh year rental profit $2,400
Estimated 5% interest for one year $1,528
Put this year's profit into a RRSP.
At the end of the eleventh year you have $40,622 in cash!

YEAR 12

At the start of the twelfth year you have $40,622
Twelfth year rental profit $2,400
Estimated 5% interest for one year $2,095
Put this year's profit into a RRSP.
Total at the end of the twelfth year you have $45,117 in cash!

YEAR 13

At the start of the thirteenth year you have $45,117
Thirteenth year rental profit $2,400
Estimated 5% interest for one year $2,319
Put this year's profit into a RRSP.
At the end of the thirteenth year you have $49,836 in cash!

YEAR 14

At the start of the fourteenth year you have $49,836
Fourteenth year rental profit $2,400
Estimated 5% interest for one year $2,555
Put this year's profit into a RRSP.
At the end of the fourteenth year you have $54,791 in cash!

YEAR 15

At the start of the fifteenth year you have $54,791
Fifteenth year rental profit $2,400

Estimated 5% interest for one year $2,803
Put this year's profit into a RRSP.
At the end of the fifteenth year you have $59,994 in cash!

YEAR 16
At the start of the sixteenth year you have $59,994
Sixteenth year rental profit $2,400
Estimated 5% interest for one year $3,064
Put this year's profit into a RRSP.
At the end of the sixteenth year you have $65,458 in cash!

YEAR 17
At the start of the seventeenth year you have $65,458
Seventeenth year rental profit $2,400
Estimated 5% interest for one year $3,336
Put this year's profit into a RRSP.
At the end of the seventeenth year you have $71,194 in cash!

We are almost done and the figures are starting to look pretty amazing. This is very simple stuff and anybody can do it – all it takes is patience and the willingness to make it work.

YEAR 18
At the start of the eighteenth year you have $71,194
Eighteenth year rental profit $2,400
Estimated 5% interest for one year $3,623
Put this year's profit into a RRSP.
At the end of the eighteenth year you have $77,217 in cash!

YEAR 19
At the start of the nineteenth year you have $77,217
Nineteenth year rental profit $2,400
Estimated 5% interest for one year $3,924

Put this year's profit into a RRSP.
At the end of the nineteenth year you have $83,541 in cash!

YEAR 20
At the start of the twentieth year you have $83,541
Twentieth year rental profit $2,400
Estimated 5% interest for one year $4,241
Put this year's profit into a RRSP.
At the end of the twentieth year you have $90,182 in cash!

YEAR 21
At the start of the twenty first year you have $90,182
Twenty first-year rental profit $2,400
Estimated 5% interest for one year $4,573
Put this year's profit into a RRSP.
At the end of the twenty-first year you have $97,155 in cash!

YEAR 22
At the start of the twenty-second year $97,155
Twenty-second year rental profit $2,400
Estimated 5% interest for one year $4,573
Put this year's profit into a RRSP.
At the end of the twenty-second year you have $104,476 in cash!

YEAR 23
At the start of the twenty third year $104,476
Twenty third-year rental profit $2,400
Estimated 5% interest for one year $5,287
Put this year's profit into a RRSP.
At the end of the twenty-third year you have $112,163 in cash!

YEAR 24
At the start of the twenty fourth year $112,163
Twenty fourth-year rental profit $2,400
Estimated 5% interest for one year $5,672
Put this year's profit into a RRSP.
At the end of the twenty-fourth year you have $120,235 in cash!

YEAR 25
At the start of the twenty fifth-year $120,235
Twenty fifth-year rental profit $2,400
Estimated 5% interest for one year $6,075
Put this year's profit into a RRSP.
At the end of the twenty-fifth year you have $128,710 in cash!

Now that this calculation is finally done let's look at several things that have happened in your favour.

1. You now have an RRSP retirement pension that did not cost you one cent of your own money. You did not have to put away any money towards it every month – your tenants did this for you. You now have around $128,710 put away. *WOW!*

2. The first house that you purchased and have been living in is, after a twenty-five year amortization period, completely paid for. *WOW!*

3. The second house that you purchased and rented out for the last twenty-five years is now also paid for with a twenty-five year amortization. *WOW!*

4. The new value of each house would be, based on averages:

YOUR ORIGINAL HOME

Original cost	$295,000
5% growth per year	$ 14,750
Multiplied by 25 years	$368,750
NEW VALUE	**$663,750**

YOUR SECOND HOME	
Original cost	$295,000
5% Growth per year	$ 14,750
Multiplied by 25 year	$368,750
NEW VALUE	**$663,750**

New appreciated value house #1	$663,750
New appreciated value house #2	$663,750
RRSP – retirement saving plan	$128,710

TOTAL NET WORTH $1,456,210

ALMOST ONE AND A HALF MILLION DOLLARS...

ALL PAID FOR!

And remember that house #2 and the RRSP's did not cost you any money... your tenants paid that for you!

This is not rocket science. All it takes is consistently doing the right thing every month, without exception. And just how much did you contribute over the last twenty-five years?

Well, the two down payments came to $18,000 plus your personal mortgage on your first home ($917 monthly x 300 payments) = $275,100 + $18,000 = $293,100 total cash you laid out including interest.

These are not huge numbers when you look at one year at a time but when you look at the over all picture, they are great numbers – over a million dollars net worth.

Remember this!

Buy and sell to create cash quickly. Buy and hold to create wealth for your estate.

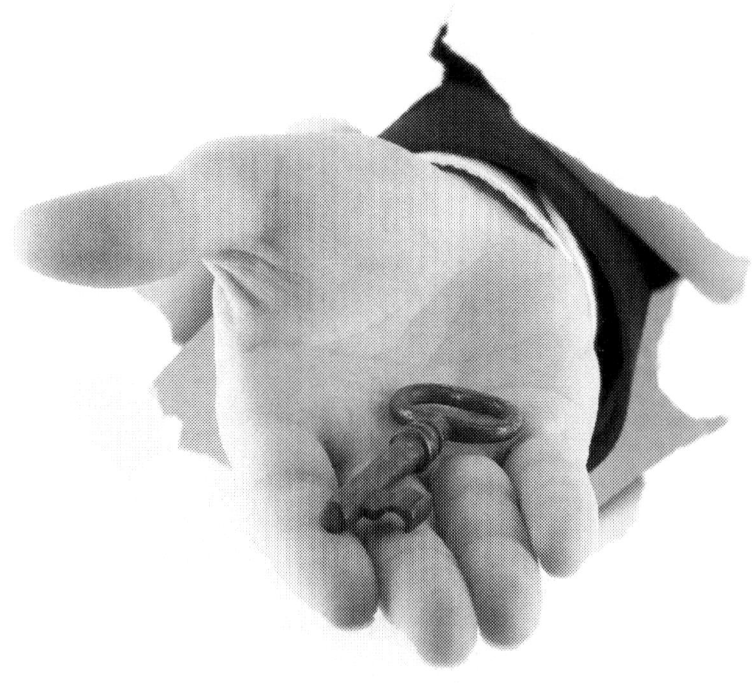

CHAPTER FIVE

YOU – THE INVESTOR PART 3

COMMERCIAL REAL ESTATE AND SMALL BUSINESS OPTIONS

COMMERCIAL REAL ESTATE

One of the best investment's in today's real estate market are shares in large multiplex units. Big apartment buildings in good areas, in good shape, and with excellent cash flow. I highly recommend considering these deals as they are bricks and mortar so no one is going to be running away with your investment.

These kind of investments usually offer huge pride of ownership because you can brag about it or show it off, as well as reaping the benefits of high returns – usually over 10%. Not only will your property value go up every year, your share value also grows every year so you are getting paid twice.

BUYING COMMERCIAL OR MULTIPLEX UNITS

My personal experiences of buying commercial or multiplex units has taught me not to bother with all those fancy formulas they mention in real estate seminars or books. They're too complicated.

My advice is
never pay more than seven times
the gross annual income.
Period.

I multiply the gross annual income of a building by seven and that's my highest offer. That's not necessarily my starting offer – you have to know what you want to pay going into the deal.

With commercial property, you must look closely at the return on the cash you just invested. This is referred to as the cash on cash return. Most books look at what the down payment was against your annual profit. True, one has to provide the down payment – but there are also legal costs, disbursements, and sometimes an appraisal cost or professional inspection fees which you also have to pay for. These costs must be included in reviewing your cash on cash returns.

THE CAP RATE

Capitalization rates, a.k.a. CAP rate, are calculated by dividing the net operating income (NOI) by the asking price (or final sale price). A lot of investors use this to quickly determine if this property is a good deal or not. This is not the only tool to use and I do not particularly like to use it at all. For example, a multiplex building with a NOI of $250,000 and selling at $3,570,000 would have a CAP rate of roughly 7%. Is this a good deal? Well, there is more to it than that.

Is the building in a really high demand area or on the slummy side of town? Is it well looked after or in poor state of repair? Is the building well cared for but aging and in need of major repairs in the very near future, such as a new commercial roof or hot water heating system? CAP rates are just quick points to tell you if a building is worth taking a closer look at. **I won't even look at any building unless is shows at least a 9% CAP rate.**

When you see a building that you are interested in, start out with a mild offer somewhere in the middle of what they are asking and what your final offer will be. Then hit them up with a home inspection, which always finds something wrong with a commercial building and allows you to go back and renegotiate for a lower price because of the cost to fix whatever the problem is.

Let's look at an example.

Asking Price $3,570,000
Gross Annual Income (GAI) = $395,000
Net operating Income (NOI) = $250,000
CAP rate = $250,000 divided by $3,570,000 = 7% cap rate showing from seller

Using my formula:
Final offer = (GAI) $395,000 x 7 = $2,765,000
New Cap rate based on my final offer = (NOI) $250,000 divided by $2,765,000 = 9% cap rate

Remember this is where you want to end at in your negotiating – it's not your starting point. If you don't reach a 9% CAP rate, it will be very difficult for the complex to cash flow properly and would be a gamble I would not recommend. The numbers have to work in your favour every time!

THREE KEY POINTS

First! Ignore the asking price. Ask for financials first. What is the GAI and the NOI? (Do your calculation.)

Second! Evaluate the overall property – the location, bus route, grocery, banking, shopping access, etc. What's the neighbourhood like? What is its income level? If the house is run down, what work is needed? Estimate the costs needed to bring the property up to your status which will help reduce the asking price. Do your calculations two or three times to make sure you don't make any mistakes. Take into account the cost of any repairs or upgrades and call a professional (electrical, plumber, fire code specialists) to get an estimate for these repairs.

Third! Always use a home inspector. I guarantee they will always find something even if it is small. All the local inspectors will make sure the building complies to codes.

It seems that when interest rates are low, multi-unit owners want more money for their properties (as low as a 5% CAP) because their returns are higher and they are not as interested in carrying any kind of vendor take back mortgages. During these low interest periods, a lot of buildings are taken off the market because the return on investment (ROI) is very good. When mortgage rates are higher, more buildings become available for sale because their ROI is not as high and owners are more willing to sell with an 8% CAP or higher. They are also willing to carry a substantial Vendor Take Back Mortgage, usually at the same rate as the first mortgage.

Remember this!

Your profit in real estate is made when you BUY not when you sell!

OPENING A SMALL BUSINESS

Let's say you have saved up a little money and feel like you want to open a small business. The first thing you need to do is your due diligence – find out all the information and costs involved to start your venture. It's essential to go over your concept and figures at least a half a dozen times and ideally, consult a mentor or advisor before you sign or start something. Take lots of time. A high percentage of businesses fail after the first year – about 90% of them. The main reason is that they are not well planned. One of the decisions you'll face is choosing between a franchise or opening an independent store. Let's take a look at them both.

FRANCHISES

Franchises do work. Their brands get advertised on television and in magazines, and they draw in customers. I know this from my days as a franchisee with Dairy Queen.

However, franchises are quite expensive to get into, and you have absolutely no control over anything in your store – there's little flexibility. You can't change or modify any product of any kind in any way, shape or form. It is their system that you will be running, and the only way it will work is for you to follow their entire system to a 'T'. They are definitely not for an 'idea person' as they have a locked system in place. In a way, the franchisor is like your mentor.

Franchise operations are proven to be much more successful than independent ones by a large margin. In fact, the figures that I have seen put them in reverse of each other: 90% success rate for franchise systems, and 90% bankruptcy or closing rate for independents.

Why such a dramatic difference? Franchises have a proven track record – and a following. The independent starts from square one and usually needs time (and money) to grow.

THE BIG BENEFITS OF FRANCHISING ARE:

• *The trade name is nationally recognized, as is the style of the building.*

• *They have an ongoing, very large advertising campaign.*

• *All the research and product development has been done. Training from head office is normally supplied so their system is understood.*

• *Ongoing support is given.*

• *Franchises usually have company benefits like dental and optical.*

• *They donate to charities which raises their community profile.*

• *Upon opening a new franchise, customers immediately recognize the brand.*

• *The quality of the product and service is usually consistent and very good.*

• *Cleanliness is a priority and controls are in place to keep waste to a minimum.*

• *Franchises usually get better locations than independents because a plaza or mall owner will give preference to them.*

INDEPENDENT STORES

You definitely need to be a 'big ideas' person with lots of skills to open your own store. Independents offer tons of flexibility and are cheaper to start up. However, they will test your imagination which is also your biggest advantage over your competition.

Rule number one:
LOCATION! LOCATION! LOCATION!

What is the visibility and exposure of your location?
What is the condition of the roof, electrical, plumbing, heating, air conditioning and washrooms?
Do you have enough parking and is it in good condition?

Is your building handicap accessible?

With commercial property it is entirely up to you to renovate, but all leasehold improvements are tax deductible. Usually you have to sign a lease and give first and last month's rent, but you can always negotiate the price per square foot. You are responsible for the renovations and whatever you fasten down (even though you paid for it) belongs to the landlord.

What will it cost to bring your building up to specifications required? Make sure your building is up to code before opening – contact the fire department and city hall planning department. Are there any environmental issues with your products or your building that could pose problems? Make sure the zoning is in place for you to operate your kind of business in that location.

FINANCING CONSIDERATIONS

FORMULA FOR BUYING A BUSINESS

Depending upon the type of business and the assets, use the lowest figure of either a) or b) below, less 10%.
a) 1 x the annual gross income
OR
b) 2.5 times the annual net income

ARE YOU BUYING

a) assets? OR
b) goodwill? OR
c) cash flow? OR
d) any combination of the above?

Get professional advice from your team.

Projecting sales is one of the hardest things to do when opening an independent business. Make it realistic otherwise you'll get frustrated and make the bank nervous. Once you have all your costs for rent, equipment, labour, and advertising, you need to have a professional business plan and a budget drawn up, or at least approved, by your accountant. If you are going to get a bank loan, this is mandatory, because all banks require some kind of pro-forma or budget set in place so they can see your opening and day-to-day operation costs and profit forecasts. Once you are open for business they will be watching you very closely to see if you are on budget. If you are falling short, the bank might call in their loan early. Business loans usually don't go longer than 15 years and banks prefer 10 years if no real estate is involved. Keep an eye on your bank loan and make sure you never miss a payment. Business insurance is an absolute must.

When starting out always stay within your budget. Do not go over budget on anything because this will put you in a vulnerable spot and you could end up short of cash for an unexpected emergency. Believe me, there will be lots of those running a business.

Cash flow is the most important part of your business because without it, you can't pay your bills, and that is not a good situation to be in. Don't buy something because it is cute or would look nice. Ask if it is going to generate cash flow!

MARKETING YOUR BRAND

Your biggest hurdle as an independent business owner is building sales from scratch – and working with a small advertising budget. In my opinion, it is worthwhile to advertise your grand opening – to show what makes you unique. First impressions matter and you only get one chance to create a good one. Using social media platforms such as Facebook, Twitter, and YouTube are free and effective marketing tools that you should embrace.

Marketing your product is extremely important because without sales you do not have a business. Try your best to market your product everywhere you can and don't be afraid to ask for advice from your mentor or hire a marketing company to get you started.

ACCEPTING CREDIT CARDS

You should be aware of the merchant machines to process Visa, MasterCard, and American Express. These machines will let your customers use their credit cards but be aware that credit card companies charge you on every transaction – 2 - 3% of your total sales. Some retailers raise their prices 2 or 3% to compensate for this loss. Some businesses, especially coffee shops, don't accept credit cards because the amount of the sale is too low per customer. Obviously, if you are selling a big ticket item you have no choice but to accept credit cards, because nobody walks around with wads of cash in their pocket.

ONLINE ADVERTISING

If you have something to sell (and don't we all?) set up a blog or website. Using google adsense is one way to keep connected with links and make money from your site. Google ads are automatically generated and you can make a few cents when a visitor to your site clicks on these ads. It's not high return, but it is a quick and easy way to make some money by putting some advertising on your site. You may want to hire a consultant on how to use Google Adwords. Once you are experienced, you can sell your expertise by consulting others how to advertise by pay per click.

Some companies that offer pay per click are:
www.googleadwordspayperclick.com
www.payperclickguru.com

www.ppcnetwork.com
www.mivapayperclick.com
www.overturepayperclick.com
www.yahoosearchmarketingpayperclick.com

Banner advertising can be a good investment for driving traffic to your website as well. These ads are typically placed near the top of a website page. When a visitor clicks on this banner ad they are directed to the advertiser's website.

There are literally hundreds of online classified ad sites where you can place your products or affiliate products for sale. Check out: *www.kijiji.com, www.craigslist.ca, www.tradepoint.ca,* and *www.classifieds.yahoo.com*

PRINT ON DEMAND

If you are planning on publishing and selling a book, print on demand or ebooks are great options. Avoid expensive printing costs and storage considerations. Set up a paypal account and get going! Print copies to order (see *www.blurb.com* for example) or charge for your ebook – a PDF which you email to your customer. It might not look as great, but it's the content that is important. Also, you don't incur any shipping costs.

USEFUL LINKS

TO HELP YOUR BUSINESS

A valuable site for helping businesses:
www.guru.com and *www.wholesalematch.com*

Registering your domain name:
www.godaddy.com and *www.cheapregistrar.com*

To increase traffic on your site, to advertise your site and improve your SEO presence: *www.engineseeker.com*

To find the best product to sell: *www.terapeak.com*

Importing from China: *www.chinaimportsecret.com*

Importing from the Orient: *www.alibaba.com*

Recommended reading for writing a condensed business plan:
The One Page Business Plan: The Fastest, Easiest Way to Write a Business Plan by James T. Horan

Do you have a great business link you'd like to share?
www.easymoneysmarts.ca

CHECK LIST AND WATCH POINTS
FOR OPENING YOUR OWN BUSINESS

Make a list of questions before you meet a professional to ask for advice. Don't be afraid to ask about risks and the down side of things. Take notes and if you have more questions by the time you get home don't be afraid to call or email back.

Take into account the simple day-to-day part of the business. Do your homework – find out absolutely everything about your type of business before you get involved. Research your product. Don't get into a dying product like video home rentals. Your product needs to have a long future.

Who is your competition and how could you improve on what they do?

Have you done enough marketing to let the public know who you are and where you are? Who is your audience?

The quality of your product and service must be down to a science and be perfect all the time. Consistency is huge in the service industry.

What is the most cost effective time to open and close the shop? Never be late opening or close early – this could cause you to loose repeat customers.

How many employees will you require? Where will you find them? Do they require a uniform? Can you tap into a government subsidized work program to help offset payroll? You need to build a motivated team, create a positive work environment, and show good leadership. This might involve taking a management course. Make sure you have safeguards in place to limit staff theft.

Do you have all your suppliers on track for delivery, price breaks, and returns? Don't waste energy or over produce. Do you have controls in place? Watch out for little things that could erode your profits. Consider buying used equipment and shop around for the best prices.

Use professional help for accounting and legal matters. Don't take the cheap road on these services.

Consider investing into a coach or mentor. They are there to help you become successful. That is their mission. *(See Chapter 9)*

"In God we trust –
every one else pays cash."

BELIEVE IN YOURSELF!

K.I.S.S. is an old adage for Keep It Simple Stupid but is still relevant for successful companies. It stands for keep it simple stupid or keep it simply simple. Don't complicate things when selling to the public. Keep your web page simple, not fancy or complicated. The same principle applies to advertising – keep it simple, and it will be effective.

Have a plan and try your very best to accomplish it. Keep repeating your dreams to yourself, bring out your humble pebble to help you get emotionally and mentally charged. Don't get discouraged by small failures – use them to become even more determined to succeed.

You are only best when you do your best!

To be really successful you need to feel hungry with a desire to be successful. Believe me, this hunger will motivate you to do things that others only dream about, and that's how it happens. It's not a miracle, it's just believing in yourself and setting your mind to get you there. The truly successful people in the world will give you the same advice – believe in yourself completely!

CHAPTER SIX

YOU – THE INVESTOR PART 4

OTHER INVESTMENT OPTIONS

FORECLOSURE AND POWER OF SALE

In a foreclosure the bank takes the property, resells it and keeps all the equity. With a Power of Sale the owner gets to keep any left over equity after the bank sells the property. Pre-foreclosure is when a third party rescues the owner by paying the arrears – in exchange for becoming a joint owner of the property. This type of deal is not for the weak of heart or the overly zealous who simply wants to steal houses. You must be a good communicator and negotiator to gain people's confidence. Convince them that you are there to truly help, not to take advantage of them.

To operate in pre-foreclosure, you will need readily available cash, either in the form of credit cards, bank lines of credit or old-fashioned savings. You will also need good credit in case you have to step up and apply for a mortgage. Cash is needed to pay off arrears until you can refinance the house. That is when you get your money back. You can make good money if the distressed people want to sell the house right away. If not and there is enough equity, get them to sign an agreement that in a certain period of time (say two years) they will refinance and pay you out 50% of equity as originally agreed. Or you can put a second mortgage that is due in two years.

Have your lawyer put this agreement in place and get it signed by all parties involved. The homeowners are happy because all their bills and taxes get paid and they get to keep their car and furniture. They might even get to keep some money and most importantly, their credit is still in good standing.

You can solicit pre-foreclosure deals by placing small signs around the neighbourhood: "Call if you are considering a foreclosure." When they do call, you must tell them that you are there to help, not to steal their house. Be sincere and treat them with the utmost respect. You will be rewarded for your efforts and they usually will split the equity 50/50 with you. Try to put yourself in their shoes and imagine how you would feel and react. It is a very sensitive area where you can actually help people and make good money without ripping them off or degrading them. We are all human and sometimes circumstances are beyond our control with nobody to blame.

There are lots of reasons why people get into these situations:
1. They lost their job
2. Their personal business is failing
3. Divorce
4. Death of an owner
5. Health issues
6. Job transfer with no company support
7. Out of town ownership
8. Some sort of financial crisis and everything falls apart
9. Mortgage rates increase – owners purchased with little down and when interest rates increase they can't afford the payments

The most powerful thing you can do to help a distressed homeowner is to help take away the stress and pressure they are feeling every minute of every day. Put a stop to the awkward and embarrassing situation ASAP by helping them keep some of their equity and providing a speedy solution to their foreclosure. Offer advice on what they should do next, and help them save their credit, and not let it get any worse.

Here are possible steps to land a successful pre-foreclosure deal:
1. Advertise with local real estate people, or place a classified newspaper ad.
2. Meet with distressed people and clearly identify the exact problem. Get the whole story.
3. Obtain all the preliminary numbers and liens on everything.
4. Make sure address is accurate on distressed property.
5. Negotiate contract and release.
6. Go to existing lender and try to renegotiate new financing or try a mortgage broker.
7. Work, or co-ordinate, with a lawyer.
8. Satisfy defaults with new financing but pay directly to the bank

or mortgage company – never give funds directly to the distressed homeowner.

REHABBING

Rehabbing can be risky investing because you have to purchase the home cheap enough, renovate it, and still make a profit on the resale. It requires money for the down payment plus the cash to be able to pay for all the renovation work. If you under estimate the costs of the renovation you will not be able to get your money back out of the house right away if you try and flip. You may be stuck with the home for a few years, renting it out during that time.

You need to run your numbers over and over again to make sure they are correct and that you did not forget anything. Rehabbing works best in a hot market. One piece of advice here is to always stick to safe neighbourhoods in middle class areas.

However, if you do everything correctly – from buying the house at a very cheap price to getting all your costs to come in under or at budget level – then you can make good money on the resale.

RENT-TO-OWN

Another real estate option is called the Rent-to-Own. This involves working with people who have bad credit (for whatever reason) but have a steady job and income. You buy a fixed up, middle class home in a good area, or you fix it up. Then you put an ad in the local newspaper advertising home for sale on a Rent-to-Own basis. Specify the address and time you are showing it. Leave a pre-recorded message on your phone saying the following:
a) you require the first and last months rent (e.g. $1600/month),

b) plus a security deposit of whatever amount you feel is appropriate (e.g. $8,000.00).

So the total needed to Rent-to-Own this home is $11,200, which is required immediately upon signing say a two or three year lease – with part of the monthly rent going back towards the down payment. As part of the deal the future owners must maintain the property 100%.

Make sure you get enough rent to cover all your costs like insurance and taxes, plus a little to make a small monthly profit for yourself. You will be dealing with people who just happen to have bad credit – maybe from a divorce or some other reason. They can't mortgage a home right now because of their credit predicament, but they are willing to pay slightly higher than average rent because they are going to own the home. Also, they usually have no problem looking after the repairs because the house is theirs.

When you buy the property make sure you demand that the seller pays all closing costs. Period. Have the 'renters' sign an agreement to purchase the home (say in two years) at a figure already established. At 8% a year interest your profit on a $200,000 home over two years would be $32,000. Less legal expenses and the monthly amount allotted towards down payment (say $100 per month for two years) $2400.

However, I have two cautions with this program. One is that when you purchased the home and did repairs to spruce it up, these costs will be more than what you are initially collecting from the prospective buyer on day one. This means you are out of pocket up front.

Secondly, what happens after two years if the people still do not qualify for a mortgage? Are you going to evict them? Are you going to extend their lease? And what happens if they decide they do not want the house and demand their deposit back? The way I see it, Rent-to-Own is a good deal only if everything goes well – otherwise it's risky.

LEASE OPTIONS

Another interesting real estate concept is called Lease Options. You do not put out any money, but these deals are hard to find. Basically you have to find a homeowner who's home is paid for, is ready to retire, and wants a fixed income. He/she rents you his/her house, (for example, 3 years with the option for you to purchase at the end of your lease), and you give him/her post-dated cheques. You then re-rent the home for more money per month than what your lease is – the overage is 100% profit for you. The trick here is that you Rent-to-Own the deal to new tenants who will pay more because they will end up with the home in 3 years (these people always will pay more monthly rent because of the opportunity). So you are collecting more money every month on the rent, and you get a bigger deposit for first and last months rent. You get a deposit from your Rent-to-Own tenants when they purchase the home. Plus, they look after all minor repairs. In your tenant agreement you specify the value of the home that they are buying, with say, a 5% a year markup – so you end up with a 15% profit on somebody else's home!

Let's say you make an extra $250 per month for 3 years – that's $250 x 36 months is $9,000 plus, let's say, it is a $250,000 home that you resell at a 15% mark-up over the three year period. That is $37,500 more profit you will get on closing. Make sure your contract allows you to resell at any time so on closing you can have it close directly into your tenant's name. That way it will save you closing costs.

The beauty of this deal is you did not put any money down and yet you earned $9,000 plus $37,500 which equals $46,500 in three years without spending a dime or risking your own money.

You may have to subsidize your tenant on a monthly basis if they are doing all the repairs and maintenance, but at the end of your agreement you should be able to walk away with around $40,000 profit without investing a dime. These deals are out there, but they are hard (but not impossible!) to find. Just imagine if you were able to do ten of these deals – that's $400,000 profit without investing any of your own money.

AN IMPORTANT DETAIL IN REAL ESTATE INVESTING

What matters most is not the cost of financing, how you get the down payment, or how much the renovations cost – the single most important thing is how much you pay for the building!

If you over-paid for a building, it will be hard to get your money back in a good market and completely impossible to get your money back in a poor market. It is critical to negotiate the entire deal so you are 100% happy with it. You need to know the end price you would pay for the building before you even start to negotiate the price. Use all the tricks in the book to get the price down. Such as requiring a home inspection, because a home inspector will always find something wrong with the home, guaranteed. Then you can come back to the homeowner and say the roof needs to be repaired immediately and that this will cost say $3500. So you tell the seller that you will pay them $4000 less than your original offer and you will look after the roof. Also make sure you (or your realtor) always states in your offer that the seller pays for your closing costs (as well as everything else you negotiated).

HOW BANKS LOOK AT REAL ESTATE DEALS

Based on my experience here are things I've noticed when dealing with banks:

1. Because cash flow is number #1 – really think about revenue.

2. Collateral, or the property itself, is number #2.

3. Your credit is number #3.

4. I do not recommend gas station property as environmental issues are expensive to deal with and most banks don't like them.

5. Stay away from restaurants in general – considered very high risk.

6. Be careful with student housing as it's difficult to get good financing – or it's usually at higher rates of interest.

7. Never buy a vacant commercial building – it's too difficult to finance.

8. I do not recommend no name motels as they are classified as very high risk.

9. I don't recommend mixed-use buildings – a commercial on the main floor and apartments on top. While these types of buildings offer good cash flow, I have found them very hard to resell and refinance.

10. The Canadian Government offers small business development money in the form of loans or grants to further business education, and wage subsidies to help new companies offset their payroll, equipment and even real estate. You can contact them at www.bdc.ca (this is with the Government of Canada).

INVESTING IN FARMLAND

Farmland always intrigued me but I found it too complicated just to dabble in. For instance, when dealing with 'Farming for Dairy', the financing is secured by the quota or a combination of quota and farmland. Also, financing will only go from 65% to 75% of the value of the farmland depending upon the shape it's in, the livestock, as well as your net worth. Amortization can only run for 15 years. Payments are flexible and can be made monthly, quarterly, semi-annually, or annually.

With 'Farming for Agricultural', you can get an agricultural line of credit which deals with seasonal fluctuation of cash flow. Most institutions will allow interest only payments and security varies, depending upon the amount requested, the risk involved and your personal net worth.

Both types of farming come under the Canadian Agricultural Loans Act (CALA) – a federal government guaranteed program for farmers and farm co-operatives. Here you can purchase real estate, livestock and equipment, as well as construct new buildings, purchase crop storage condominiums or consolidate farm debt.

Farm property line of credit is good for up to 75% of the value of the farm property. Once you apply and are approved you never have to reapply.

With a rural property mortgage the amortization is good for up to 30 years and 75% of the value of the farmland. This is not to be confused with a Rural Property Line of Credit which is designed for individuals who have their primary residence on agriculturally zoned land (greater than 5 acres), but whose main source of income is 'off farm'.

As mentioned, it's all pretty complicated for the Average Joe.

REAL ESTATE CONTRACTS

Contracts are a huge part of any real estate deal. Never sign anything unless your lawyer looks at it first and do not be afraid to tell someone that "I am not signing anything until my lawyer looks at it first." Remember, whoever controls the paper controls the deal. Whoever controls the deal has complete control over the outcome and the money.

A contract consists of several elements such as the offer and the acceptance of the offer, written documentation with legal descriptions, and the signatures of principals involved. There can be add-ons to the contract, or side agreements (commonly referred to as addendums), but they should have all the same aspects as the original document. I recommend you use addendums as much as possible because they always supersede the main contract agreement.

Some examples of addendums are:

• *Purchaser wants seller to pay all closing costs*

• *This agreement is subject to the buyer obtaining a building inspection that meets their level of satisfaction within the next 15 days*

• *This agreement is subject to the buyer obtaining suitable financing within the next 20 days*

• *Purchaser has the right to assign this agreement to any corporation, person or entity at his/her sole and absolute discretion at anytime before closing*

• *This agreement is subject to the purchaser obtaining his/her partner's approval to this agreement*

• *Purchasers deposit can only be cashed upon removal of all conditions*

• *This offer is subject to the purchaser viewing property 24 hours before closing*

BUYING PROPERTY IN THE U.S.A.

A WORD OF CAUTION

Much of our population is retiring and the surge will be getting bigger as the baby boomers get older. In or around the year 2030 there will be a population shift, in particular with Canadians moving to warmer climates like Florida, Texas, Utah, Arizona, Nevada, California, South Carolina and North Carolina.

Right now would seem be a good time to be investing in property in these areas as prices are at unbelievably low levels. Once the markets pick up again, these prices will bounce back quickly.

Buying property in United States can be a bargain right now with the current economic conditions, but Canadians need to be aware that they are considered foreign investors.

The U.S. government has imposed a 100% tax hike on all homes owned by foreigners. For example, a typical Florida coastline condo with property taxes at $2,800 annually would cost a Canadian double this amount, or $5,600 annually. That's huge and you really need to consider if it's worth owning with high maintenance costs.

Will you be able to sell this property if the U.S. government does not lower the taxes to the new purchaser, even if they are American? There is no guarantee they will even consider it. Once taxes are set it is almost impossible to lower them. You could be stuck with a property for a long time, or forced to 'give it away' close to cost. It seems like just a big headache. There are lots of better investments out there.

CHAPTER SEVEN

LEARN HOW TO GET A CAR ...FOR FREE!

How about if I showed you how to get a free car? Yes, a FREE car, all paid for. This will not work for everyone, as you need to secure a business loan. However, for those of you that can, and want a free car, here is how to get it.

Borrow $50,000, at say, 5% interest over seven years on a regular loan. Then walk across the street to an investment company (Edward Jones for example) and invest this $50,000 at say 8½% compound interest for seven years.

In seven years your money is now worth approximately $85,000. That's a $35,000 capital gain with no tax in Canada.

$2,500 in interest charges per year are tax deductible because your loan is for business. You can get $1,000 tax refund (at 40% tax rate, which will vary) so $1,500 is your actual cost (interest less tax refund) x 7 years = $10,500

The $35,000 profit, less the $10,500 interest cost, gives you a $24,500 profit to go out and pay cash for a $24,500 car.

Technically, the bank is buying the car free and clear for you over the seven years. You did not have to use a dime of your own money. If you want a bigger car, then get a bigger loan if you can afford to do so. Rates and time frames will vary, but this gives you the idea.

Talk to your accountant before doing this.

CHAPTER EIGHT

MY BUSINESS STORY

Twenty-seven years ago I opened the first video rental superstore in south western Ontario, Canada. It was located on a ¾ acre property in downtown London and I owned the building as well as the business (called Video Lease). In the store, I also put in a coffee shop and placed an antique car inside the building. I was open 24 hours a day seven days a week. Government programs helped me hire my employees.

One day I decided to throw a big sale and offer all movies for just pennies. My idea was to stand out from the crowd and get lots of publicity. I promoted with flyers, newspapers, and magazine ads, but my most effective advertising was with the local radio stations. I actually hired all three local stations for the day of the sale, paid them about a thousand dollars for one day's promotion, tipped the announcer and bought everybody lunch. It cost me a small fortune. The DJs plugged us every 10 minutes throughout the day, and I asked Coke and Pepsi (both!) to donate product in exchange for their names being continuously mentioned. In anticipation of a record crowd, I also decided to hire the local police for the day to control traffic, which turned out to be a great idea. I had all my staff ready and hired a few extra people for the day (and it still was not enough). My sale worked so well I couldn't believe it. People were lined up down the street. I was thrilled.

I did a lot of the job myself, but I also had a terrific management team. You need a team to assist you all the time – even though you don't necessarily think so. When you are first starting this journey, your key team member is without a doubt, your personal coach and mentor. More about this in the next chapter.

I have owned several small businesses and I made a lot of money. One of my favourite and most lucrative business was a cleaning company – it was not your average cleaning company. I had some experience cleaning offices to help put me through school. I was an aggressive worker and always took pride in myself and my work, and never left a job until I was satisfied that it was done properly – whether the clock had stopped paying me or not. I was just that way because I knew it would be a reflection on me personally. So, I came up with a plan on how to make a lot of money in the cleaning business. My goal was to make my life better by working smarter, not harder.

I went out and got cleaning contracts by putting on a tie and presenting a professional plan. Then I sold the rights to service these accounts (sub-contract out the cleaning) – but still owned the contracts. I would invoice the accounts, deduct a 20% royalty fee, and pay the sub-contractor. The sub-contractor had to do all the work, as well as supply all the equipment and cleaning supplies. I then placed a small ad in the local classifieds and sold my sub-contracts for a large sum of money.

I realize now that if I had a mentor I could have reached my goals years earlier. Day by day I could see progress, no matter how small it was. I kept telling myself that if I took it nice and slow and built a rock solid foundation, I would make it to the top. I could envision myself getting there by laying bricks in my mind, day by day. I kept laying more bricks (in my mind I was building a large skyscraper) and as each day passed I was getting closer to the top. And you know what? It worked! While at the time it seemed forever, within six months I had enough money to invest in real estate.

Even back then I had a vision board to help me build my dream – to reach out to do better and more. I found that I really enjoyed my work and never thought about what time it was because I was happy. Slow but steady was my motto, just like the story of the turtle racing the hare.

We can learn from this story because it shows how humans are. We don't need magic or a sophisticated scheme, just guidance to keep us on the slow and steady path. Our day will come.

Buying or running your own business is very different from just investing in real estate. With a business you can put your personal touch into it and make it part of you, and that is very rewarding. I have always believed that if you are honest and work hard to please your customers, you will be very successful. Put some imagination into it – don't be afraid to be creative and express your self through your business. You will be amazed at what this creativity will do for you as it reflects back into your business and your cash register.

Always remember no matter what the situation is in your life – it's how you deal with it that matters most. If you want a good outcome try to stay positive and cheerful and the outcome will be better for everyone involved. As long as you are focused on your life goals and you have support in your hand from your humble pebble, you can make the best of any situation.

Smile. Life is a journey and you always want to take the smooth road because with less friction you can reach your destination faster.

F13
ins
help
del

CHAPTER NINE

EASY MONEY SMARTS MENTORING PROGRAM

To make a change you need to be emotionally strong in order to keep negativity out of your mind and around you. You absolutely have to have the desire to achieve your dream. Many people are lazy and would rather watch television or just sit around and do nothing. They believe they can't reach their goals so don't bother trying. Their attitude is negative and they lack commitment.

Ever wonder why diets don't work? People who need to be on a diet need to drastically replace their bad eating habits for good ones. It is the same thing with money. You need to change your bad money habits for good money habits. To achieve this you have to be committed and surround yourself with positive reinforcement.

A mentor will reinforce you positively and coach you to be your best. Most professionals and sports figures have coaches who help them be successful. Financial mentoring is no different. People often ask advice from someone who is inexperienced. How can you expect to get ahead with amateur advice – 'the blind leading the blind'!

WHAT TO EXPECT FROM A FINANCIAL MENTOR

A financial mentor will help launch your new, healthy financial life.

Imagine having someone in your life who is skilled, experienced, and non-judgmental – who really cares what happens to you, financially and otherwise. Your mentor will get to know you as a person – where you have been, what you are doing, and where you want to go. He or she will bring out your hidden talents and explore ways to help with your current job, finances and life in general. The answers to the questions in the beginning chapters of this book will help your mentor get to know you – in the strictest of confidence, of course.

It is difficult to be objective about yourself. Your mentor will provide the skills to see your big picture – your highest self. Your fears and passions will be taken into account, and you'll be helped in reaching your goals. You'll be shown what risks are involved and how you can minimize them. A mentor will not tell you what you MUST do, they will show you the options so you can make a clear decision.

Expect to talk on the phone to your mentor once a week for about half an hour. It's advisable not to skip an appointment or be late. Why hold back your progress and waste your money? Remember that you are not your mentor's only client – respect your contract. Expect to be given homework – things to accomplish. If you don't work at it how do you expect to succeed?

It's also motivating to take this financial journey with a close friend, especially if you both have mentors and can compare notes. Maybe you will even discover the inner passions or dreams of your friend!

BENEFITS OF WORKING WITH A FINANCIAL MENTOR

You will become better with your finances.
You will be more productive.
You will find yourself doing more than you would on your own.
You will find yourself being more effective and more focused.
You will become more balanced and fulfilled.
You will be assisted to make better financial decisions and investments.
You will be on your way to financial success!

THE EASY MONEY SMARTS MENTORING PROGRAM

Easy Money Smarts offers two mentoring programs. One is for individuals, and the other is for business professionals. Both programs are priced per month, and include 2 to 3 hours of coaching per month. A minimum thirteen month contract is required.

With mentoring there are no guarantees – the mentor is your coach but only YOU can make it happen. You are accountable for how much you achieve. I can though, guaranteed that you receive the best support for you to achieve your goals. Your mentor will offer guidance and professional help every step of the way, so you will never feel alone or uneducated in your business decisions. It is in Easy Money Smarts best interest to make sure every mentor relationship is successful, not only in business, but also in your overall life.

IT'S EASY TO JOIN!

www.easymoneysmarts.com

Jim has always acted with the utmost integrity. He is the kind of person that you could entrust with any task and know that it would be completed on time, on budget, and most importantly, on target.

Ron Van Rooyen, BA CFP PA

FAQ'S ABOUT MY MENTORING PROGRAM

1. Why would anyone need a personal coach or mentor when I only make a little over minimum wage?

A mentor will work with you to get you to a higher level of income. He or she will help you eliminate debt, start saving and put you on the path to good investments. Without financial mentorship, chances are that years from now you will still have no savings or investments – because we are creatures of (bad) habits.

2. Are there any guarantees that I will make more money?

Of course not, but it is in my best interest for you to succeed! Easy Money Smarts will work with you, diligently and honestly, but you must also do the work. We are committed to helping you but you need to be committed to helping yourself. We can show you quicker ways to get results, but you need to follow your mentor's plan.

3. How long does a mentoring program last?

A mentoring program typically lasts for 13 months minimum. Your mentor will work with you for 2 to 3 hours a month online. Most people need that constant coaching to keep them on track. It is very easy to slip back into bad habits but your personal coach will keep you motivated and on track – that is their job!

4. What can I expect to gain from joining the EASY MONEY SMARTS MENTORING?

For everyone it will be different. If you have a lot of money toinvest we can direct you into high yielding and secure type of investments (especially for those retirement-aged). For people stuck in a rut, we have different plans depending on their situation. First, we try to get you out of debt, then start you on a savings plan so you can eventually start making investment choices and start turning your life around in a positive and happier way. Our goal is to make you successful and happy.

5. When can I start to see results?

Almost immediately after joining. You'll be shown how to raise your income almost immediately, along with a plan for changes. Mentoring works. Just follow the program and you will not be disappointed. Every month things will improve as long as you stick to the plan.

6. Finances are a serious matter, so why do you inject some humour throughout your material?

Because humour helps relieve stress and can put us back on track after a tough day, or situation. With humour, you can you made people feel good, even just for a moment. Laughter seems to build confidence. It's motivational. People are always attracted to something humorous. It's wonderful stuff.

7. What if I don't have a college or university degree. Can I still make this work?

Absolutely! We work with everybody, at all levels. This is basic stuff. You do not need to be a rocket scientist to make this work, and our coaches are down to earth with real life experiences. If, for some reason, you do not understand what has to be done, don't be afraid to ask your coach to go slowly through it again and even put it in writing. We work at your speed. The Easy Money Smarts mentoring programs is designed to make you successful. We want you to fully understand what you are doing, so after the mentoring program is finished, you can carry and use us for occasional support. Your mentor is there for as long as you need them, even if that means extending your program for a few extra months if necessary.

8. Should I tell my friends and family that I am trying your system or just keep it to myself?

Tell the whole world about it! Because they will be watching to see if you are successful and staying true to what you are doing. This will be positive and motivational for you. However, beware of the negative people out there that are always skeptical or jealous – they will try to bring you down. Totally ignore them: they are not going anywhere – you are. Stay with your real friends who will try and keep you positive and support you. If they see you being successful, they will want to join you and see if this works for them too. You could make them part of your weekly coupon team and delegate who researches what sectors for great discounted deals. These friends will also appreciate hand made gifts from the heart more than anybody. This could be a huge bonding between you and your friends and family. This is never ending stuff – searching for deals and making gifts together. It almost seems old fashioned, where real value came from the heart not the wallet.

9. What books would you recommend that I read?

Tuesdays with Morrie *by Mitch Albom*
Awaken the Giant Within *by Anthony Robbins*
7 Habits of Highly Effective People *by Steven Covey*
All these books focus on people, their habits and the power of motivation.

CHAPTER TEN

USEFUL BITS

DIFFERENT BUSINESS STRUCTURES

THE BEST TIME TO INVEST

ECONOMIC CYCLES

THE INTEREST LADDER

TERMINOLOGY

DIFFERENT BUSINESS STRUCTURES

A. SOLE PROPRIETORSHIP

Where the owner is in complete control of the business and makes all the decisions about running the company. This kind of business is easy to set up and has the advantage that the owner gets all the profit along with a lot of tax write offs as business expenses. The bad side to sole proprietorship is that the owner is completely responsible for all debts and mistakes.

B. PARTNERSHIPS

Where two or more people join together to start a business, and usually combine assets and talents towards making the business work. Normally decisions are made together and both share any liability. The partners are taxed individually and can write off certain expenses as deductibles. This type of business formation is relatively easy to set up but the difficulty with a partnership is that the partners may not always get along.

C. LIMITED PARTNERSHIP

This kind of set-up is excellent when a group of investors are considering pooling their money to make a large purchase such as a multi-million dollar apartment building. The number of partners is unlimited but usually a specific number are allocated for one project. Each partner is not personally liable for the partnership's debt or obligations. You are taxed on your earnings separately. Any transfer of interest usually requires the general partners approval, which protects your investment as well.

D. CORPORATION

With a corporation you are a shareholder and the only risk is your investment. There is no other liability. Corporations sell shares to raise capital. Usually there are two kinds of shares: the common share, which usually carries voting rights, and the preferred share, which usually carry no voting rights. With voting rights, only 51% of the vote is required to get a motion passed, or a majority on any decision. Votes can be mailed or done by proxy. In smaller limited companies, a minute book is kept by either the company lawyer or accountant and yearly financial records and meetings are documented and entered. These recordings in the minute book are not open for public viewing.

Note: All taxpayers in Canada are given a tax exemption with a lifetime maximum of $750,000 on capital gains on the sale of shares of a Canadian controlled private corporation (C.C.P.C). A C.C.P.C is taxed at approximately 20% on the first $500,000 of active business income each year. A C.C.P.C. must have less than 50 share holders and be Canadian controlled.

THE BEST TIME TO START INVESTING

There is an old saying that I am sure everyone has heard at least once: "I wish I knew what I know now when I was twenty". And it is so true! We get smarter and more experienced the older we get but wouldn't it have been wonderful to have all this knowledge and experience at a younger age?

Ideally the best time to start investing is when you are in your early twenties because you have many years to watch your money compound with interest. The actual amount put away does not have to be large because the power of compounding is enormous. You would be earning interest on your interest and interest on your compound interest and even more interest on your compound interest-interest and so on till it gets to be huge. Time is money and when it is compounding. It's like a giant snowball – it just gets huge.

Remember the story about working for a penny for the first hour and doubling it every hour thereafter.

FIRST DAY OF WORK
1 cent for first hour of work
2 cents for the second hour of work
4 cents for the third hour of work
8 cents for the fourth hour of work
16 cents for the fifth hour of work
32 cents for the sixth hour of work
64 cents for the seventh hour of work
$1.28 for the eighth hour of work

SECOND DAY OF WORK
$2.56 for the ninth hour of work
$5.12 for the tenth hour of work
$10.24 for the eleventh hour of work
$20.48 for the twelfth hour of work
$40.96 for the thirteenth hour of work
$81.92 for the fourteenth hour of work
$163.84 for the fifteenth hour of work
$327.68 for the sixteenth hour of work

It did not take long before the amount was staggering. Within two days you are earning over $327 an hour on a job where you started out at only a penny an hour. This is how the principle of compound interest works – and it's staggering.

ECONOMIC CYLES

Inflation (the expansion phase) and recession (the shrinking phase) are the two main recurring phases. Government tries to protect us from depression or economic crisis by increasing their spending in order to keep the wheels of the economy going, and having social programs in place such as welfare and employment insurance.

Economists use an index of leading indicators to gauge exactly how the economy is doing. Some of the main economic indicating factors are the jobless rate, the number of new houses being built, sale orders of consumer goods from factories, and the stock market.

History teaches us that the economy, interest rates and profits operate in a cycle. Which goes from boom to bust and back again. However we never know how long these cycles last.

In the end it is up to you to look after yourself by investing in what you are comfortable with, whether it is a small business, franchised system, limited partnership, or real estate.

"Take calculated risks. That is quite different from being rash."

George Patton, 1885-1945 American military leader

THE INTEREST LADDER

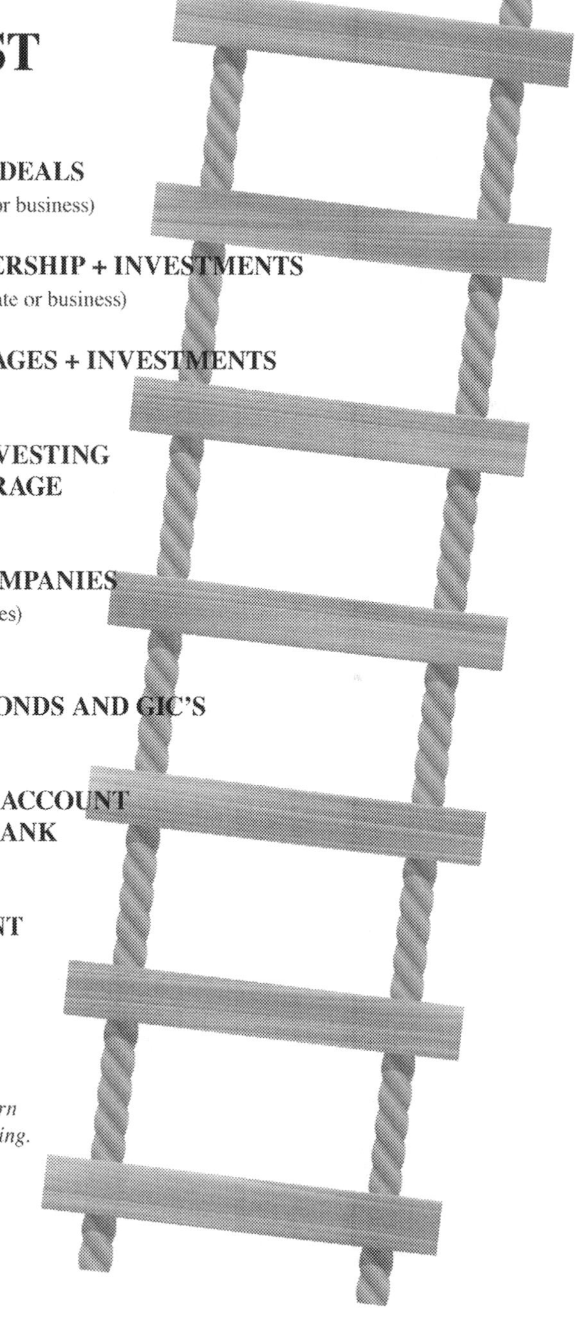

THE INTEREST LADDER

JOINT VENTURE DEALS
25+% return (real estate or business)

LIMITED PARTNERSHIP + INVESTMENTS
10-16+% return (real estate or business)

SECOND MORTGAGES + INVESTMENTS
10-14+% return

REAL ESTATE INVESTING ON YEARLY AVERAGE
8-10% return

INVESTMENT COMPANIES
(for example, Edward Jones)
5-8% return

GOVERNMENT BONDS AND GIC'S
3-5% return

NO TAX SAVINGS ACCOUNT AT ANY MAJOR BANK
1-8% return

SAVINGS ACCOUNT AT A BANK
¼-½% return

Note: All figures are approximate rates of return and are constantly changing. This is just an example.

TERMINOLOGY

THINK & ACT SUCCESSFULLY AND PROFESSIONALLY. BECOME FINANCIALLY LITERATE!

1ST MORTGAGE
The first mortgage document registered on title of a property.

2ND MORTGAGE
The second mortgage document registered on title of a property behind the first mortgage.

3RD MORTGAGE
The third mortgage document registered on title of a property behind the first and second mortgage. The higher the mortgage figure, the higher the risks of not getting your money back.

ABANDON
To give up or yield the rights usually to a property. To let it go voluntarily, usually in the case of bankruptcy.

ACCOUNTANT
One professionally trained in doing financial bookkeeping and addressing tax assessments.

ADDENDUM
Something to be added. A condition, which supersedes the original contract but is still part of.

AGREEMENT
A contract legally binding two or more parties. (Verbal agreements are not legally binding in real estate.)

AMORTIZATION
The paying down of a mortgage with regular principal and interest payments over a certain period of time. Usually after 25 year amortization, the mortgage will be completely paid off.

APPLICATION

A form to be filled out about your personal situation or property you are purchasing for mortgage disclosure or insurance requirements. Must be personally signed for acquiring a mortgage.

APPRAISAL

A local licensed appraiser's expert opinion on the value of a property. Usually showing comparable properties in your neighbourhood that have recently sold.

APPRECIATION

An increase in a property value over time.

ARREARS

A payment of debt that is outstanding or overdue. Usually means an account is not paid or is behind on its payments.

ASSESSMENT

Evaluation used by taxing authorities to calculate property or income taxes.
Property assessment x millrate = property tax payable
Income assessed x tax rate = income tax payable

ASSET

Something a person or corporation owns of recognized value that can be used to borrow money against. Usually real estate or vehicles.

ASSIGN

To nominate or appoint for a specific purpose.

ASSIGNEE

A person who has been given the right to act in place of another.

ASSIGNOR

The person who transfers the right to another person.

ASSIGNMENT CLAUSE
A clause in a contract that allows the purchaser to transfer interest to another party orentity.

ASSUMABLE MORTGAGE
Where purchaser is allowed to take over the sellers mortgage without any changes to the mortgage.

AUDIT
The verification of any financial records for personal or business use. Following of a paper trail.

BANKRUPTCY
Financially unable to pay one's bills and whose real property the courts will administer. Insolvency.

BEACON SCORE
Your credit score.

BREAK-EVEN POINT
When you are not making or losing money.

CAPITAL
Cash money available now.

CASH FLOW
Short-term flow of cash and working capital for business or real estate.

CAVEAT EMPTOR
Legal meaning for "let the buyer beware" message.

CHARGE
A legal document that sets out the terms of a mortgage.

CHATTEL

A piece of property other than real estate that is usually movable and not deemed to be fixtures.

CLOSING
When a property transfers ownership from a seller to a purchaser, usually done at lawyer's office and registered at a government office (Land Titles or Land Registry office).

CLEAR TITLE ON DEED
Free of any encumbrances or liens and shows legal ownership.

CLOSING COSTS
The total of the expenses, in addition to the cost of a property: land transfer feeds, legal fees, document registration fees, etc.

COLLATERAL
Other property or asset of true value owned by a borrower and lent or secured to guarantee another loan.

COMMERCIAL
Not for your personal use. Usually apartment complex or retail or offices. Generates income in form of rents.

COMMISSIONS
Fees charged by agents or brokers. Paid by the seller.

CONSOLIDATE
To unite into one system or whole.

CONTINGENCY
Any condition that must be fulfilled or completed before a deal can close.

CONTRACT
An agreement that binds two or more parties to do certain things before they can receive compensation. Should always be checked by a lawyer.

CONVENTIONAL MORTGAGE
A regular mortgage that does not exceed 80% of the property value.

CONVERT
To change to a new status. For example, from an apartment to a condo.

CONVEYANCE
The transfer of property from one person to another.

COVENANT
To enter into formal written agreement about some form of real estate and its use.

CREDIT BUREAU
Agency that keeps track of your credit record.

CREDIT REPORT
Comes from a credit bureau agency and details where you live and work, and your past credit history including bankruptcy, late payments and your beacon score.

DEBT TO INCOME RATIO
Used by banks and mortgage companies. Expressed as a percentage when you take a borrowers income and divide it by their expenses.

DEED
A legal description of a property in exact detail. Proof of ownership.

DEFAULT
Failure to carry out an obligation. Commitment has not been met.

DEPRECIATE
To go down in value over a period of time.

DISCHARGE OF MORTGAGE
This is a document that indicates when a debt has been removed from the title of a property.

DISCLOSURE
To reveal everything in detail, good or bad, about a certain property.

DOWN PAYMENT
A pre-determined amount the purchaser pays on closing to a lawyer, usually by a certified cheque.

DROP SHIPMENT
A shipment of goods sent directly from a manufacturer to the client. When selling online, many manufacturers will ship a product you sold directly to your customer.

EASEMENT
A right of way to make use of another's property. Usually is registered on the property title.

E-BUSINESS
Business on the internet – buying and selling goods or services.

ENCUMBRANCE
Any burden, responsibility or obligation that restricts freedom on a parcel of land. Usually it is registered on the property title.

EQUITY
The value of a property after deducting any charges to which it is liable such as a mortgage or taxes.

ESCROW
A formal contract or deed, which does not come into effect until some specified condition has been fulfilled or completed.

EVICTION
To recover a property by lawfully removing the occupant – usually for non payment.

FICO SCORE
A credit score similar to a Beacon Score.

FIDUCIARY
Held or given in trust.

FIRST RIGHT OF REFUSAL
The first chance to purchase the property at a later date. Hard to enforce and can be easily manipulated. To be enforced, it must be registered on the title.

FIXED RATE
An interest rate that remains the same for the term of a mortgage, but not the life of the mortgage.

FLIPPING
The buying and selling of a piece of real estate over a very short period of time.

FORECLOSURE
The seizure of property for failure to make payment of a mortgage or loan.

GDS (Gross Debt Service Ratio)
A calculation used by banks and mortgage companies. The principle plus interest, plus taxes, plus 50% of condo fees, plus heating, then divided by your gross income. Should never be higher than 32%.

GAI (Gross annual income)
Amount of money earned before taxes.

HARD MONEYLENDER

Private moneylenders who make real estate loans for higher than normal interest, usually to people with poor credit history.

HIGH RATIO MORTGAGE
A mortgage that is higher than 80% of the property value.

INVESTOR
The person who puts up all the money.

JOINT VENTURE
Two people getting together to buy real estate. One person puts up the money (the investor) and the other person does all the work and management. When the property or business is sold the profits are typically split 50/50.

LANDLORD
The owner of a rental property – whether residential or commercial. The person to whom the tenants pay their rent.

LEASE
A rental agreement where the leasee agrees to pay the leasor a certain amount of money over a certain period of time.

LIEN
The right to hold another's goods until a claim or payment is settled.

LINE OF CREDIT
A set credit limit, usually from a bank, that allows the borrower to withdraw money up to that limit.

LOAN TO VALUE
The total of the loan against the value of the property.

MARKET VALUE
The going rate for a piece of property at a certain time. Fluctuates year by year with the economy.

MENTOR
A personal coach who helps you reach your goals and bring out your talents and passions. Or a person you model your life or career after.

MORTGAGE
Secure loan against the value of a property.

MOTIVATED SELLER
A seller who will do anything to get rid of their property, such as holding a mortgage or reducing their price.

NOI (NET OPERATING INCOME)
The income that is leftover after deducting the operating expenses from the income, but does not include mortgage payments.

NOTICE OF DEFAULT
A notice form the lender that payment is in arrears.

OPTION TO PURCHASE
An option in an agreement that gives you the right to purchase a property at a specific price within a certain period of time.

POWER OF ATTORNEY
The written consent authorizing another person to act on their behalf. Should only be granted after legal advice by a lawyer.

POWER OF SALE
A court action used by choice by a lender upon default of payments by a borrower.

PROFIT AND LOSS STATEMENT
A financial statement from a business showing its incoming revenue, outgoing expenses and net profit or loss.

REFINANCE

To obtain a new loan or mortgage by paying off the old loan or mortgage.

REVERSE MORTGAGE
Is an interest accruing mortgage that is usually only repayable upon the death of a homeowner or upon the sale of the property. Normally done with retired people.

SELLER FINANCING
Also referred to as VTB or vendor take back. The current owner of a property sells the property to a purchaser, but the seller takes back a mortgage on the property at a set rate of interest, usually the same as the going rate for first mortgages.

SPAM
Electronically sent messages on the Internet, usually unwanted. Similar to junk mail. Can be blocked.

TDS (Total debt service ratio)
All your debt divided by your gross income. Should never be more than 40%.

TERM
Refers to a period when a mortgage must be fully repaid or renegotiated. Most people do 5-year terms over a 25-years amortization period, but it all depends on the going interest rate and your personal situation.

VARIABLE RATE
An interest rate that fluctuates over a period. Usually aligned to the bank's prime rate.

VENDOR
The seller or owner of a property.

JIM W. MATHE

Entrepreneur Jim W. Mathe is author of *Easy Money Smarts* and creator of *Easy Money Smarts Seminars* and *Mentoring* programs. A former franchise operator, Jim now invests in real estate and businesses. He holds a university degree in Business Administration and decided to become a money coach to fulfill his love of helping 'The Average Person' to become financially successful.

www.easymoneysmarts.com